A Vice-President of the Society of Dorset Men, Colin Pomeroy was born and brought up in Weymouth. Educated at the former Weymouth Grammar School, he was a member of the local Air Training Corps squadron as a teenager and was in possession of a pilot's licence before having a driving licence.

Colin served in the Royal Air Force from 1960, flying Shackleton and, then, Nimrod aircraft at home and abroad, until retiring as a Squadron Leader in 1980 and embarking upon a new career as an airline pilot. With over 11,000 flying hours under his belt, a serious illness forced early retirement upon him in 1987 and he now assists in the running of his family's fish farm and lakes at Pallington Lakes, near Dorchester in Dorset.

As well as working on two books about Weymouth with Maureen Attwooll, *Weymouth Century* and *Weymouth Revisited,* his other books include *Isle of Wight Railways, The Bermuda Railway, Gone - But Not Forgotten!, Military Dorset Today, Discover Dorset: Castles & Fort,* and *The Flying Boats of Bermuda.*

Front Cover Photograph
A fascinating aerial view of Weymouth Harbour,
dated sometime during the period 1925 to 1928. Vessels which
can be identified include the paddle steamers *Albert Victor*
and *Emperor of India,* whilst just beyond the (old) Town Bridge is the
cargo vessel *Reindeer.* Alongside the Pavilion Theatre, lies one of the
Channel Islands service passenger vessels – either the *St Patrick* or *St
Helier.* Note the goods train passing beneath the Town Bridge.

Following page
Three Westland Wallace aircraft from No 6 Armament Training School
at RAF Warmwell in close 'Vic' formation above Wyke Regis in 1938.
The road and rail bridges linking the mainland to Portland is clearly
visible behind them. The lead aircraft is a Mk 1 Wallace, distinguished
by its open cockpit. Virtually all of the open countryside below the
aircraft has now been built over.

Wings Over
WEYMOUTH

Colin Pomeroy

THE DOVECOTE PRESS

One of the most historic flights in the history of aviation:
Short S38 hydroplane lifts off from *HMS Hibernia* in
Weymouth Bay, May 1912.

First published in 2005 by The Dovecote Press Ltd
Stanbridge, Wimborne Minster, Dorset BH21 4JD

ISBN 1 874336 77 6

© Colin Pomeroy 2005

The author has asserted his rights under the Copyright, Designs
and Patent Act 1988 to be identified as author of this work

Designed by The Dovecote Press
Printed and bound in Singapore

All papers used by The Dovecote Press are natural, recyclable products
made from wood grown in sustainable, well-managed forests

A CIP catalogue record for this book is available
from the British Library

1 3 5 7 9 8 6 4 2

Contents

Introduction

IN 1990 I was visiting my son who was working in Bermuda and, being interested in railways, spotted the islands' 'Railway Trail' footpath and set out for Hamilton Library to find a book on the Colony's former railroad. There wasn't one – so I decided to write it, and thus *The Bermuda Railway. Gone – But Not Forgotten!* was published in 1993.

The gestation of this book is similar. In the introduction to his most enjoyable book *In Dorset's Skies*, the author Colin Cruddas regrets that amongst the omissions from the book is, with some other minor sites, the airfield at Chickerell. I again set out to remedy this deficit – and what follows, including a lot more about the local aviation scene than I had originally planned, is the result!

Hot air balloons graced the skies over Weymouth during Victorian times. Initial powered-flying activities in the area took place from airfields at Lodmoor and later at Chickerell – with both of them operational together during the 1920s and early 1930s – and from Royal Navy warships.

Aircraft from these early years of aviation required only the minimum of facilities and very short 'runways' from which to operate. Additionally, there are still local folk with memories of occasional flights from a variety of other impromptu sites, such as those at Redlands and Southill – near, in both of

DH3 Fox Moth in the ownership of Sir Alan Cobham at Chickerell, almost certainly in August 1931. The young girl alighting from the cabin is Elsie Neal (later Rodenhurst); the schoolboy ahead of her – short trousers and school cap so typical of the period – is unidentified, but certainly appears to have enjoyed his flight!

Supermarine Southampton MkI S1037 within the confines of Portland Harbour on 20th September 1926. This aircraft was at that time based at RAF Calshot, Hampshire on the strength of No 480 Flight, which on 1st January 1929 became No 201 Squadron, RAF.

Seen here at RAF Sharjah in the Trucial Oman States (now the United Arab Emirates) in 1967, this Coastal Command Avro Shackleton Mk 3 of No 206 Squadron, RAF Kinloss, is typical of the aircraft using the Chesil Beach Bombing Ranges during the 1950s and 1960s.

these particular cases, to Lodmoor and Chickerell respectively. It would seem that more pleasure flying took place in the 1920s from Lodmoor than it did from Chickerell, for it is flights from the former airstrip which are far more often recounted today than those from Chickerell.

After the Great War, during the final year of which planes based at Chickerell flew anti–submarine missions, Lodmoor and Chickerell each played host to air circuses. From 1937 onwards Chickerell and its associated Chesil Bank Bombing Ranges fulfilled important training functions in support of the Allied war effort in the Second World War – an ongoing support which continued into the Cold War days until 1959. During the desperate years from 1939 until 1945, the local skies saw major activities, ranging from the defensive engagements of the Battle of Britain to the offensive actions associated with D–Day and, later, Operation Market Garden. Such actions have been eloquently reported elsewhere and will not be covered again within these pages, save as passing references.

In the post war years local skies echoed to both piston and jet engines, as aircraft used the Chesil Beach Ranges and Royal Navy helicopters flew from Portland's HMS *Osprey* Naval Air Station until its closure in March 1999, the surface shipping Naval Base itself having already been closed down in 1995 when the pennant of Flag Officer Sea Training was transferred to Devonport.

Weymouth's annual carnival regularly sees the RAF's Red Arrows gracing the skies above the town, with other front line aircraft occasionally showing their lines to locally appreciative audiences. In 1980 I myself was lucky enough to be able to fly Nimrod MR Mk1 XV262 of No 42 Squadron in display over that year's carnival crowds on my last operational flight in the Royal Air Force.

Overflights by vintage aircraft of, for example, the RAF Battle of Britain Memorial Flight and the RN's Historic Aircraft Flight often give poignancy to the veterans' events, of which Weymouth and Portland

A fine view of a Nimrod, XV255 off the Cornish coastline. The weather was not a bit like this in August 1980 when we returned to St Mawgan from Weymouth, the airfield being shrouded in low cloud and mist. I almost suffered the embarrassment of having to divert on my final flight – and miss the champagne!

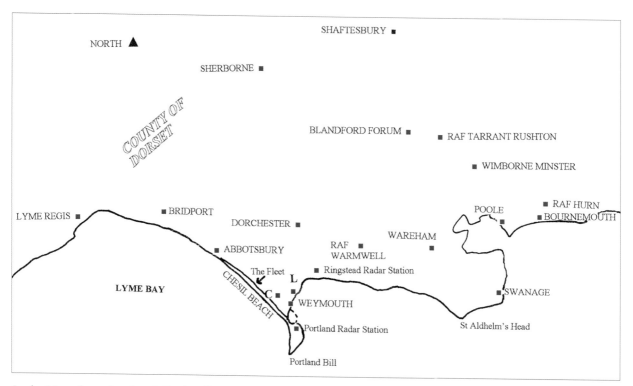

In the Map above the site of Chickerell airfield is marked 'C' and that at Lodmoor marked 'L'. Note also the location of the airfield at RAF Warmwell, seminal to the story of the bombing ranges in Lyme Bay,

are justifiably proud, but otherwise the skies overhead are generally quiet.

One unusual visitor put in an appearnce on 18 July 2003, when British Airways Concorde G–BOAE under the command of Captain Les Brodie flew a low farewell over the town as the airline's supersonic transport fleet prepared for retirement – over 25 years after the first commercial SST flight from London/Heathrow Airport on 21 January 1976. G–AE was returning to Heathrow on a routine test flight after maintenance inputs and had rendezvoused with the liner QE2 for a photo opportunity off the south coast.

Meanwhile, an appreciable amount of aviation associated 'high tech' manufacturing takes place locally, most especially on the Granby Industrial Estate – the site of the former Chickerell airfield.

I sincerely hope that this book will bring back fond memories to those who have been in any way associated with the local aviation scene – either actively or as a passive observer – and will indicate to those of more recent years the importance, in its own small way, of aviation in the twentieth century in this corner of the beautiful county of Dorset.

Now no longer 'Queen of the Skies' – the Concorde supersonic transport airliner over Weymouth Town Bridge just four months before British Airways' last SST flight on 24 October 2003.

ONE

The Early Years

Undoubtedly the Weymouth and Portland area is best known for its associations with the sea. But it was – as we shall see – an historic aerial event in Weymouth Bay which brought sea and air together, leading marine aviators along the road of development which today sees the nuclear-powered aircraft carrier as the main weapon in the arsenals of the major powers. The success of the aircraft carrier owes much to the three British inventions [in addition to the ski ramp for VSTOL operations] which have revolutionised fixed-wing carrier operations since the end of the Second World War: the angled flight deck, the steam catapult and the mirror landing aid.

Ballooning over Weymouth

However, the earliest recorded local aviation activity is the ascent on the evening of 12th August 1842 of the experienced balloonists a Mr Green and Captain R.W. Currie in the balloon *Albion* from Weymouth racecourse, at Lodmoor. This was probably the first flight to take place in Dorset skies – although the first hot-air balloon flight anywhere had been as far back as 1783, with the flight of the Montgolfier-designed craft in Paris by de Rozier and the Marquis

Airborne! The *Albion* over Weymouth Esplanade before drifting off towards Bere Regis. (There is some artistic licence in this picture, for the balloon's initial direction offlight after taking off was to the north east away from the town!).

This grainy photograph captures a seminal moment in the advance of military aviation: Lt Samson lifts the Short S38 off the bows of HMS *Hibernia* and into the history books.

d'Arlandes. The first recorded flight in England was that of James Sadler, with an ascent in October 1784 (also in a Montgolfier craft). Green and Currie stayed airborne for about an hour and a half, They were watched by a crowd of over 12,000, reached a maximum altitude of some 12,000 feet, and came back to earth near Bere Regis.

November 1855 saw another recorded balloon ascent from the Weymouth area, when a Mr John Vine carried out one (and possibly as many as three) flights in a Montgolfier-designed balloon, the first take-off at least noted as being from Spring Terrace, Rodwell.

All these early ascents took place in the late autumn. Providing calm conditions exist, a hot air balloon performs better in the winter than in the summer, the contrast in temperature between the hot air in the envelope and the surrounding free air being at its most marked.

Though not as historic as the 'Albion' ascent, a rather more dramatic flight is recorded as having taken place on a Saturday afternoon in 'about the year 1891', when three aviators lifted off in a large balloon from a field near to Lodmoor Hill where Lord John Sanger's Circus was performing,

presumably to advertise the show. A change in wind direction saw the balloon drifting towards the sea. In a hasty attempt to land on terra firma rather than in the water, the crew operated the release valve too soon or too excessively and ended up entangled on the spire of St John's Church on the Esplanade. Finally releasing themselves – but not without bending the weather vane to a crazy angle – the airmen landed heavily, but unscathed, on the beach between Brunswick Terrace and Greenhill. The publicity might not have been as intended, but it certainly was considerable – and capped off by having the deflated balloon and gondola taken away from the scene on a circus trailer drawn by an elephant!

Weymouth Bay's Historic First Flight

Before the storm clouds of war developing over continental Europe broke in 1914 and armed conflict ensued, and less than nine years since the Wright brothers had first taken to the skies at Kitty Hawk, North Carolina, the Royal Navy was conducting trials as to how it could best make use of aeroplanes. At the time it thought of them as the eyes of the fleet rather than, as they later evolved, weapons of war in their own right.

On the 10th January 1910 Lieutenant Charles R. Samson RN had succeeded in taking off from the stationary HMS *Africa*, off Sheerness. A stationary warship is however particularly vulnerable. Additionally, it would soon become detached from the main fleet. The Admiralty wished to perfect a system whereby an aircraft could take to the air from a vessel that was underway.

It was in Weymouth Bay, late on the afternoon of 9th May 1912, that this first took place – the vessel involved being HMS *Hibernia*, under the command of Captain Grafton which, like HMS *Africa*, was a 12" gun battleship of the King Edward VII class.

When the battleship was some three miles off the Portland Harbour Breakwaters, and heading towards them at some 5 knots, Lt Samson was launched over the its bows from a wooden platform on the foredeck. He flew over the Breakwaters, across Weymouth Bay, finally landing at the eastern end of Lodmoor, adjacent to where the town's local racecourse was once located.

The aircraft involved was a Short S38 'amphibian' (which would in those days have been known as a 'hydroplane'), a pusher biplane carrying the serial number T2 and fitted with a 70 hp Gnome engine. It was one of two such aircraft belonging to the Naval Flying School at Eastchurch in Kent, with another two dual control models [an S43 and an S44] later being operated by the Central Flying School at Upavon, Wiltshire. Essentially a seaplane, the S38 had wheels incorporated in the floats to permit the aircraft to alight on land as well as in the water.

Samson's flight was a major historic event by any standards – although it was necessary for the aircraft to land alongside the *Hibernia* to be craned back aboard. It was not until August 1917 that the first deck landing was achieved, when Squadron Commander E.H. Dunning landed his Sopwith Pup on the flight deck (which had no arrester wires) of HMS *Furious*. Sadly Dunning lost his life five days later when attempting another landing on *Furious*.

Samson, however, was more fortunate and rose to the rank of Air Commodore in the, still at that time to be formed, RAF. He formed and commanded No 3 Squadron of the Royal Naval Air Service – which still exists today as No 203 (Reserve) Squadron of the Royal Air Force, flying search and rescue Sea King helicopters. He also fought in the ill fated Dardanelles Campaign, and was an innovative aviator in anti-submarine and anti-Zeppelin warfare. He died in 1931.

Above Wearing the largest of grins, Lt Samson strolls nonchalantly away from his Short S38 aircraft at Lodmoor after his notable flight on 9th May 1912.

Below With part of the launch ramp above the A Gun turret clearly visible, the Short S38 is recovered back aboard HMS *Hibernia* after one of its successful flights. To this day the term 'recover aircraft' is used when referring to the readying of a carrier to land-on her aircraft.

Earlier in the week, prior to his flight from the *Hibernia*, Samson had flown off the directly off the water in more 'conventional style'. Here we see him on 6th May becoming airborne in an S41 biplane. At this time the aircraft carried the serial code 'H1', but it was later designated as aircraft number '10'.

At much the same time as Samson's early flights, another naval officer – Lt Spenser Grey of HMS *Agamemnon* – was carrying out trials from Lodmoor. In his case the aircraft involved was a Blackburn Mercury III monoplane The aircraft was built specifically for Grey, and first flew on Christmas Day 1911, but had no serial number allocated to it. Earlier the Royal Navy had given some thought to building a large dock at Lodmoor, but this was dropped and some 40 to 50 acres of the land were instead rented from the owner for aviation purposes.

The Home Fleet Review

Another early brush with flying also occurred in May 1912, when the renowned aviation pioneers Claude Grahame-White and Benny Hucks came to Weymouth to participate in the review of the Home Fleet in Weymouth Bay. Grahame-White brought his Henri-Farman monoplane to the resort by rail, but the arrival method of his companion is not recorded. "G-W's" diminutive monoplane (similar to that used by Louis Bleriot for the first aeroplane flight across the English Channel in July 1909) was later wheeled on its own purpose-built trolley along The Esplanade and Preston Road to 'The Weymouth Cricket Club's ground at Overcombe Corner', where it was re-rigged for flight. Overcombe Corner was, by now, also becoming known as the location of the Lodmoor airstrip!

The Home Fleet was reviewed in Weymouth Bay by King George V. HMS *Hibernia* and HMS *Africa* were both present as ships within the 3rd Battle Group, and both sported their aviation ramps. A contemporary souvenir wall chart of the Review shows the two aircraft over the lines of warships.

With a beautiful old steam pinnace in the foreground and the bulk of the Isle of Portland looming menacingly in the distance, the Short S38 flies past the Royal Yacht *Victoria and Albert* during the May 1912 fleet review.

Portland Harbour's seaplane support facilities during the Great War year of 1917, with three Short 830 seaplanes pulled clear of the water for maintenance. These aircraft were later to work in conjunction with Chickerell's landplanes.

Most interestingly, the chart also marks the Cricket Club Airstrip – annotating it as 'Lodmoor. Aviation Ground and Hangars'.

The two pilots had worked together since at least 1910, when they had accompanied a Bleriot & Farnham aircraft on the SS *Cymric* to a flying meeting at Boston, USA: Grahame-White as the pilot and Hucks as a mechanic, with Hucks paying for flying lessons from his wages.

Hucks later became famous as the first Englishman to loop an aircraft, whilst Grahame-White was famous in those early days of aviation for achieving second place in the £10,000 first prize Daily Mail London to Manchester Air Race of April 1910, as the founder of Hendon Airport, and for conducting early anti-shipping bomb trials – this latter activity was another indication as to why their visit to Weymouth was made at the time of the Royal Review.

After the review Grahame-White left the local area with his aircraft by rail, but Hucks flew direct to London. He took off at 3.20 pm and arrived at Hendon at 5.51pm, giving him an average airspeed over the 142 mile route of just over 90 mph – a very creditable performance for the year 1912.

Although HMS *Hibernia* was present for the Review, a planned demonstration of her flying-off abilities for the sovereign was not carried out. Nevertheless Samson, Jerrard and Longmore all gave flying displays over the assembled warships – which were, knowing the military mind set, possibly more dramatic and than those of Grahame-White and Hucks! Operating out of Lodmoor and supported by personnel from Eastchurch in Kent, at that time effectively the centre of British naval aviation, these were probably amongst the most significant and formative flights carried out by RN pilots prior to The Great War of 1914 – 1918. So fascinated were the local folk by all this aerial activity, a strong police presence was drafted into Lodmoor for crowd control purposes.

Later in 1912 (the year in which the royal warrant creating the Royal Flying Corps was signed by King George V) it was the turn of the Army to visit the local area to exercise with the Royal Navy and to work with the fleet off Lulworth Cove. A Major Webb flew down in August from his base on Salisbury Plain – probably from No 2 Battalion of the Royal Engineers at Larkhill, but possibly from Upavon or, less likely, Netheravon.

Lodmoor and Chickerell Airfields

The records which survive today of the airfields at Lodmoor and Chickerell, Weymouth's other aerodrome in those far off pioneering days, are

An undated view of 'The Aviation Ground and Hangars' at Lodmoor, but probably some time during the 1920s – for the hangars were no longer standing when flying ceased here in the following decade.

sparse, although enough tantalising snippets exist to give us an indication of what went on in these very early days of powered flight. The excellent aviation historian the late Chris Ashworth tells us that the Chickerell airfield was originally established in 1918 as one of a series of small aerodromes set up around the coast for use by land-based aircraft operating in the anti-submarine role. Locally they would have augmented the Royal Navy's seaplane base in Portland Harbour (HMS *Serepta*) – where such aircraft as four, and later up to twelve, Short floatplanes operated from a slipway which is still visible (but unusable as the piers behind it have been raised to such a height as to make access almost impossible) and the airship mooring-out stations at Toller Porcorum, Moreton, and Upton.

On the 1st April 1918, following the amalgamation of the Royal Flying Corps and the Royal Naval Air Service, the Royal Air Force came into being as the world's first independent air force. Three months later, D Flight of No 253 Squadron of the fledgeling RAF was flying three DH 6 patrol aircraft out of Chickerell, which were replaced in August by 513 Flight of No 241 Squadron.

With the cessation of hostilities following the Armistice of 11th November 1918, the military's interest in Chickerell faded away and during the following month the RAF departed.

The Shephard Memorial

There is one, however, one particularly interesting record of the First World War left locally, which is but rarely seen – a memorial to a senior RFC officer in the form of a cut-off laminated wooden aircraft propeller. It stands, normally within a small wooden shelter, in the grounds of the 3D Education and Adventure Centre at Osmington, and bears the following dedication:

In memory of
Brigadier General G S Sheppard (sic),
DSO, MC,
Royal Flying Corps
Died
Jan 19th 1918.
R.I.P.

The memorial stands just in front of Shortlake House, once the Shephard family home, and now the residence of the Manager of the Adventure Centre. Why Shephard should be commemorated at this spot is a little uncertain, for it was the home of Lieutenant Colonel Charles Sinclair Shephard DSO (1848 – 1930), who served in the Royal Fusiliers. Probably he was a nephew, for Charles and May Shephard's only son, Hardinge Lilford Shephard, was lost at sea in 1915 whilst serving on HMS *Viknor*, and is commemorated on the Naval Memorial at Portsmouth.

The son of Sir Horatio and Lady Shephard, Brigadier General Gordon Strachy Shephard DSO MC is buried at the Lapugnoy Military Cemetery, in the Pas de Calais. In addition to his Distinguished Service Order (awarded in June 1917) and Military

The Shephard Memorial Cross, removed for clarity in our photograph from its normal protective shelter. The dedication has incorrectly spelt the officer's surname.

9th December 1915. 10 Sqn flew the standard corps reconnaissance BE2C, whilst 6 Sqn operated in both the fighter and army co-operations roles from airfields in Flanders whilst equipped with Bristol Fighter aircraft. Shephard was in attendance when the King inspected 6 Sqn, together with 5 Sqn, in October of that year.

On 1st April 1918, 4, 6 and 10 Sqns RFC became 4, 6 and 10 Sqns RAF, when the Royal Air Force was formed. Today 4 Sqn is based at RAF Cottesmore, Rutland, flying the VSTOL Harrier GR7 and 6 Sqn is based at RAF Coltishall in Norfolk flying the twin-jet Jaguar GR3 – both close support/ground attack and reconnaissance aircraft, the latter shortly due to be withdrawn from RAF service. 'Shiny Ten' is at RAF Brize Norton in Oxfordshire operating VC10K aircraft in the air-to-air refuelling and strategic transport roles. 6 Sqn will move to RAF Coningsby in 2006 to re-equip with the Typhoon, whilst 10 Sqn will loose its individual identity in October 2005 on amalgamation with 101 Sqn.

After leaving 6 Sqn, Shephard's next appointment was as Officer Commanding No 12 Corps as a lieutenant colonel. He remained there until February 1917, when he was gazetted as General Officer Commanding No 1 Brigade in the rank of brigadier general.

Gordon Shephard was recognised as an outstanding leader. Even as a senior officer he was renowned for flying his Nieuport scout aircraft over enemy lines to see for himself the situation on the ground and for getting out from behind his desk and visiting the frontline aircrew under his command

On 19th January 1918, Shephard's brilliant career came to a tragic end. He was coming in to land at Auchel, in the Nord Pas de Calais, when his aircraft was seen to spin into the ground. For a pilot as experienced as the brigadier this was quite unusual, for a spin is initiated by a stall brought on by reducing air speed below a safe level. Maybe he was tired; maybe he had a momentary lapse of concentration or his attention was drawn elsewhere in this critical phase of flight; maybe he suffered an engine failure and stalled trying to 'stretch the glide' to reach the airfield?

Whatever the cause it was a great loss, not only to the RFC but also to the nation as a whole. Had he survived the carnage of the Great War, as he could so easily have done had he taken a more typical approach to his responsibilities for one so senior, there can be little doubt that he would have achieved even greater things in the post-war Royal Air Force.

Cross (November 1915), he was also five times Mentioned in Dispatches and was Chevalier of the Legion of Honour (France). At just 32 years of age, he was the youngest officer of such rank in the British Army.

Already a qualified pilot, having learnt to fly at his own expense in 1911 and being awarded Royal Aero Club Certificate number 215 – so a true early aviator! – he originally served as an officer in the Royal Fusiliers (City of London Regiment). He joined the Royal Flying Corps in June 1913. The following year he was appointed as Flight Commander on No 4 Squadron – a unit based in France flying aerial photographic sorties in BE2Cs and RE8s for the British Expeditionary Force.

On 4th January 1915, now a major, Gordon Shephard took command of No 10 Squadron, where he continued in post until given command of No 6 Squadron on 6th March, whence he remained until

TWO

Between the Wars, the 'Flying Circuses' and the Ranges

The early post war period was one of boom for aviation. Large number of ex-military aircraft were available to entrepreneurs willing to take the risks, leading to the 'starry-eyed' establishment of many air routes, aerodromes and airlines which would have never seen the light of day had the head (or wallet) ruled the heart! For a short while Handley Page Transport Ltd operated a service between London and Weymouth (Chickerell) aerodrome using twin-engined former HP 0/400 bomber and patrol aircraft, the civilianised aircraft being known as the HP12, with a top speed of 97 mph (156 km/h), although there appear to be no records left in existence referring to these flights.

The London aerodrome used for the service was at Cricklewood, alongside the Brent Railway Sidings at Hendon and primarily Handley Page's factory airfield. It was also neither ideally located nor particularly large or well surfaced, and has the dubious claim to fame of being the location of Britain's very first scheduled air service fatal accident, an HP 0/7 crashing on take-off on 14th December 1920 with the loss of four lives.

Some six months later the last passenger service flew from Cricklewood (the new Croydon aerodrome by now having become the main airport for the London region), and it must be assumed that Weymouth (Chickerell) Airport's brush with scheduled service civil aviation ceased at about that time – or even earlier. Cricklewood finally closed to all flying in 1930: Handley Page had continued to use it up to then on company business only, and the whole area is now covered by an industrial estate.

As we have seen, the Lodmoor airfield, which at one time boasted at least two double-fronted hangars on its north-east side, was located at the eastern extremity of what is now the RSPB Lodmoor Nature Reserve. This beautiful area of marshland is rich in bird life and is obviously much changed since the 1920s and early 1930s. Weymouth Cricket Club held its home matches here (Overcombe Corner), with other uses being as tennis courts, as the venue of the Royal Counties Show in 1911 and as a racecourse in the mid-19th century.

It is interesting to note that in these days Weymouth had two departure points, for in 1919 and 1920 the Bournemouth Aviation Co was also operating a service with Avro 504s (with just accommodation for a single passenger) from its Ensbury Park aerodrome in Bournemouth to the site on Lodmoor. The company also operated a Bournemouth to Cricklewood service with an HP0/400 but, like the Weymouth service, it was short-lived and not a financial success – partly, perhaps, because it was no quicker than the rival rail service!

Canvas hangar in the south west corner of Lodmoor airfield, with the spire of St John's Church at the north end of Weymouth Esplanade, just visible beyond. The aircraft is an Avro 504K, G-EBLA.

A Fatal Crash

Amongst the more unusual incidents to occur at Lodmoor was the crash of Avro 504K G-EBLA, which crashed into Weymouth Bay on 19th June 1928, shortly after passing into the hands of A. C. Cooper from its previous owners, The North Lea Aviation Company.

Cooper had been flying his biplane at the prestigious Bath and West Show at Dorchester the previous week. On this occasion he was carrying out aerobatics about 200 yards offshore – which would then have more likely been referred to as 'stunt flying' – when he failed to pull out of an incipient spin following a series of loops, and hit the sea in a relatively flat trajectory.

Cooper's passenger, his mechanic E.F. Carpenter, was rescued from the wreckage and taken, after first aid treatment at the Hotel Burdon (now the Prince Regent Hotel), to Weymouth Hospital. But Cooper's injuries were fatal – the gallant efforts of Messrs Rule, Harvey and Webb and a naval petty officer to save him all being in vain. The aircraft was towed to the motor boat landing stage, where the pilot's body was recovered before the broken remains of the Avro were brought ashore. Ironically, there were large crowds on the seafront that day awaiting a forecast tidal wave – which never came!

The ill-fated pilot's mortal remains were taken away for burial in a Daimler hearse driven by Weymouthian Reg Bugler. The hearse broke down in the New Forest and Mr Bugler spent an

A view of Avro 504K G-EBLA before its crash. Note that there are 2 passengers in the rear cockpit. The bare hill in the background, to the east of Lodmoor, is now almost entirely covered with houses.

Resplendent in its overall blue finish, Surrey Flying Services' Avro 536 G-EBRB at Lodmoor. This aircraft was built as a 504, but widened by 9 inches to take a fourth passenger. First registered on 27th April 1927, it was written off after crashing at Barry, Glamorganshire, on 28th May of the following year.

uncomfortable night trying to sleep across the front seats – always aware of the presence of his travelling companion.

Lt Cooper, unmarried, aged just 29 and with eleven years Royal Air Force service to his credit, was buried at St John's Church, Buckhurst Hill in Essex, his home town.

Sir Alan Cobham's First Visit

When thinking of the air circuses of the late 1920s and early to middle 1930s, those of Sir Alan Cobham are the ones which first spring to mind (although Cobham himself did not like the term 'circus').

Between May and October 1929, Sir Alan (his knighthood having been awarded in 1926 in recognition of his long distance pioneering flights out

and back from London to Australia) embarked upon a personal crusade to increase the nation's awareness of aviation. Altogether, he flew some 54,000 miles around mainland Britain and the Isle of Man in his DH61 Giant Moth aircraft *Youth of Britain* (G-AAEV) in pursuit of this aim.

Sir Alan is on record as saying 'It is vital to the safety of the nation that Britain should become a nation of aviators'. He visited 110 'flying grounds', for that was what many of them merely were, as far apart as Plymouth, Ronaldsway, Dundee, Lowestoft and, probably, Weymouth and Bournemouth (for both were earmarked for a visit on his planned itinerary). He achieved the remarkable safety record for those days of carrying over 40,000 passengers on some 5,000 flights safely and virtually without incident. Sadly, with the reliability of the railways in that golden era of rail travel, there was very little overt public enthusiasm for internal air travel – especially when the potential traveller took into account the disruptive effect the weather could have on even the most routine of flights.

'The Barnardstormers'

Although Cobham probably visited the Weymouth area during his 1929 Municipal Aerodrome Scheme search for potential sites for civil aerodromes, it seems that the first actual 'air circus' event staged over Weymouth was that by C.D. Barnard's 'World's First Air Circus'. The Circus performed at Chickerell on August 4th and 5th 1931 – one of 118 towns visited between 1st April and 11th October that year. Another was Dorchester, on 23rd July, where those to enjoy the freedom of the air included the town's Mayor and Mayoress (Councillor and Mrs W.J. Fare). After their flight Mrs Fare made a most unusual presentation to Captain Barnard: a beautiful model aircraft made entirely of local flowers.

The Air Circus went under the unofficial nickname of 'The Barnardstormers', and featured a stable of aircraft as fascinating as Cobham's. Between 1933 and 1934 the Air Circus even toured India – a quite remarkable achievement by the standards of the day.

Like the *Dorset County Chronicle* at Dorchester, the *Dorset Daily Echo* (as the local newspaper was then titled) gave its readers the chance to fly for free by offering 20 tickets as draw prizes. The draw was to be made by the Mayor of Weymouth Captain F.W. Hamblin, and proved so popular that three members of the *Echo* staff had to spend several hours opening

Barnard's autogiro G-ABFZ at Weymouth on 5th August 1931. Designed in Spain and called the Cievra C19, in this case a C19 Mk IVP variant, many of the 180 aircraft manufactured were built in the UK by Avro, who called it the Avro 620 Rota. This particular aircraft later passed from Barnard's ownership into that of Cobham.

The Cievra autogiro was the first mass produced rotary-wing aircraft built.

the envelopes containing the draw coupons.

Additionally, free draws for complimentary tickets to fly with Barnard were held at the Regent Dance Hall and the Regent Theatre. Mayor Francis Hamblin and Town Clerk Percy Smallman were flown as guests of the Air Circus – although all flying was delayed on the first morning due to thunderstorm activity above Weymouth and the surrounding coastal waters.

Barnard brought a fleet of six aircraft to Weymouth. Amongst them was the 12-seater Fokker F VIIa G-EBTS in which, accompanied by the Duchess of Bedford, he had made record-breaking flights to India and Cape Town and back, and had then purchased from her for £900. The others included a Cierva C19 Mk IVP autogiro, and two Spartan three-seaters G-ABJS and G-ABET.

Also in 1931, keen to stimulate Government interest in the commercial flying opportunities which he saw on the horizon, Sir Alan Cobham brought his National Aviation Day organization into being. During the same summer that Barnard flew from Chickerell, he flew demonstration and passenger flights from Weymouth, probably from Lodmoor rather than from Chickerell.

The standard route for these passenger flights was across Weymouth Bay to the harbour, south to Portland Bill and back to the landing ground via Portland Harbour and Bowleaze Cove. The price was 10 shillings (50p) for the full trip, or just 5 shillings (25p) for a shorter route which went no further south than Weymouth Harbour. At least one local gentleman – then a lad of just 5 years old – still

has in his possession the signed photograph bearing the caption 'National Aviation Day Display' given to him as a souvenir by his pilot, Flt Lt H.C. Johnson, and certifying that he had flown with him in the DH80A Puss Moth G-ABXY *The Hearts Content*, and supported British aviation. This aircraft was the one in which Jim Mollison, husband of another aviation pioneer Amy Johnson, made the first solo east to west crossing of the North Atlantic in August 1920.

Cobham's 'Flying Circus' Returns

Cobham was a director of Airspeed (1934) Ltd, the aircraft manufacturers, and he commissioned the company to build him an aircraft suitable for his National Aviation Days – the Airspeed Ferry, of which he purchased two. Cruising speed wasn't of overriding importance, but short field performance and good visibility for the passengers were.

The Ferry was a ten seat biplane, with a 55 feet (16.76m) wingspan and a cruising speed of 85 mph (136 kph). It was powered by three de Havilland Gipsy in-line engines – in the rather unusual configuration of one in the middle of the top mainplane and the other two outboard of the fuselage on the lower mainplane.

The prototype, Airspeed's first powered aircraft, first flew in March 1932, with Cobham then going on to pay for his machines (G-ABSI [*Youth of Britain III*] and G-ABSJ) in monthly instalments of £500 – taken from the profit of his public displays and the pleasure flights of his 'Flying Circus'.

Although beyond Sir Alan's control, the spirit of national loyalty continued in the early war years when, in April 1940, G-ABSI was impressed for war service as AV968 and finally saw her days out as a training airframe with No 474 Squadron of the Air Training Corps, based at Long Eaton in Derbyshire.

Above Barnard's Fokker F VIIa G-EBTS at Chickerell on 5th August 1931. Previously known as *Princess Xenia*, and once involved in an unsuccessful North Atlantic crossing attempt, Barnard renamed her *The Spider* – the name being painted below the cockpit window. Behind stand two Spartan 'Three Seater' Mk 1 aircraft – G-ABKK (known as *Helen of Troy* from 1932 after change of ownership) and G-ABJS – with the airfield boundary in Radipole Lane beyond.

Below Ticket from one of Sir Alan Cobham's visits to Weymouth

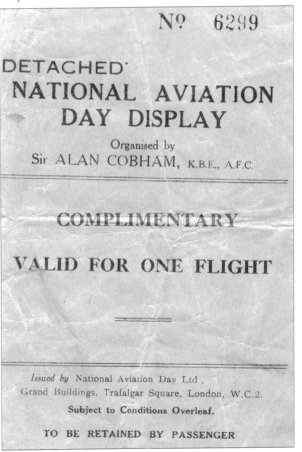

NO 6299

DETACHED
NATIONAL AVIATION
DAY DISPLAY

Organised by
Sir ALAN COBHAM, K.B.E., A.F.C.

COMPLIMENTARY

VALID FOR ONE FLIGHT

Issued by National Aviation Day Ltd,
Grand Buildings, Trafalgar Square, London, W.C.2.

Subject to Conditions Overleaf.

TO BE RETAINED BY PASSENGER

Sir Alan Cobham poses for the camera in front of his office wall chart showing his planned 1929 itinerary. Note the marker at Weymouth (and the other relatively local one at Bournemouth).

The 'Flying Circus' – which was in essence an extension of his dream of making the British public more aviation aware – visited Chickerell on at least three occasions. The first time was in August 1932, when it enthralled locals and holiday makers alike. The programme included some twenty 'daring events' and opened with a grand parade and flypast of some dozen or so aircraft. Admission to the airfield was for a nominal fee and flights cost five shillings (25p) for a flight over Weymouth and Portland Harbours in, not only, the Ferry passenger aircraft, but smaller aircraft such as the DH80A Puss Moth. In addition, other aircraft seen included Avro 504Ks, Tiger Moths, gliders and his early variant autogiro.

By all accounts, if the published programme is anything to go by, the enthusiastic spectators certainly got their monies worth:

'. . . then will come the thrills of aerobatics, in which there will be an indication of the liberties that may be taken with a machine in the air, and the wonderful control that skill and experience can alone give. In this and in other items, Sir Alan, speaking from the ground, will broadcast a description of each stunt.

There will be a bit of crazy flying during a demonstration of how not to fly, and a three-engined Airspeed airliner and a pilot will be partners in an aerial dance, with music from the ground.

An exhibition of auto-towed gliding will be followed by a race round the pylons, in which the fastest machines will take part, and other items will include aeroplane-towed gliding, parachute descent, a demonstration of the autogyro, aerial marksmanship, inverted flying, continuous rolling and wireless controlled flying.

The programme will conclude with an exhibition of aerobatics in formation.'

No mention was made of the wing-walking, carried out by a Mr Martin Hearn, nor the parachuting by Mr Ivor Price (who, sadly, was to be killed at Woodford, near Manchester, in May 1935 when his parachute 'candlesticked'. He had been married for just two weeks and his young bride was in the crowd watching his performance).

The *Dorset Daily Echo* held a competition for twenty of its readers to fly free in the Ferry, the lucky winners being chosen in a draw conducted by the Town Mayor, Captain F.W. Hamblin – who, together with the Town Clerk and members of their families, was given a demonstration flight.

Just as is the case today, aviation had its detractors in the 1930s, when, for example, shops being open on a Sunday would have been beyond belief. On the occasion of the August 1932 visit members of the Lord's Day Observance Society disrupted operations by scattering waste paper all over the airfield, which Flying Circus staff had to clear up before flying could commence.

The Society had protested against 'the proposal that Weymouth's quiet and restful Sunday should be desecrated by the flying exhibition', stating that there were six days in which people could become 'airminded' and that on the seventh they should become 'heavenly-minded'. In response the barnstormers' 'Bombing the Bride' team hurtled around Weymouth in one of the campaign cars, covered in flour from the 'bombs', and touted for trade through a megaphone, inviting onlookers to savour the delights of taking a flight or watching the stunt flying and parachute drops.

On the subject of motor cars, for his work along the south coast in 1932 it was planned that Sir Alan's entire transport system should consist of Austin cars, the Austin Motor Car Company obviously hoping that the car-buying public would assume that they had been chosen by such a famous person in recognition of

Above Just as the Royal Air Force's Aerobatic Team The Red Arrows do today, Cobham flew his display team at low level between events for the publicity it generated. With Cievra autogiro G-ABUC below the main formation, the more agile biplanes hold station on the much larger blue and silver 22 seat Handley Page 35 Clive Mk III G-ABYX, *Youth of Australia*. Main formation left to right: Avro 504K (G-ACCX), Tiger Moth G-ABUL, HP Clive, DH 83 Fox Moth (G-ACEY, *Youth of Newfoundland*), Spartan 3-Seater (G-ABYH) and a second Avro 504 G-ACLV. Cobham later adopted the name Astra for his HP35 aircraft. (Note that G-ACCX and G-ACLV were actually owned by Air Travel Ltd and attached to the Cobham team.)

Below Cobham's elegant HP35 Clive III G-ABYX in her earlier military days as J9126, and originally carrying the name *Chitral* (a state on the Indian frontier, and once a British Protectorate).

21

Sir Alan stands alongside his innovative loudspeaker van, but not at Weymouth and a Ford rather than an Austin! The nearer aircraft in the background, with a Tiger Moth behind, is Blackburn Lincock Mk II, G-AALH.

their style and reliability. However, Sir Alan is also on record as using Ford, Leyland, and Armstrong Siddeley vehicles, but not necessarily in 1932.

For Cobham's next visit to Weymouth, on 23rd August 1933, the *Daily Echo* again offered free flight tickets to its readers, but this time in a competition with a difference. On 16th August one of the Circus's aircraft was to overfly the resort between noon and 1.00 pm and to overfly Dorchester during the following hour. Readers were asked to assess the aircraft's height at the time that it turned on its smoke generator. Its height was 747 feet (an apt aviation number!), the closest estimate being an almost exact one of 750 feet.

The only recorded accident to any of Sir Alan's team during its visits to Weymouth occurred during this 1933 visit, when 19 year old parachutist Price Ward, with over 1,000 safe jumps to his credit, dislocated his foot after a heavy landing. Co-ordination of the aerial activities seems to have gone a little astray, for as Mr Ward was preparing to land

– in breezy and less than ideal conditions – he found himself on a collision course with a landing Ferry aircraft and his parachute partly deflated about 25 feet above the ground after becoming distorted by the Ferry's propeller wash. In all other respects the two shows held at Chickerell were similar in content and proved very popular with local residents and holidaymakers alike.

The next visit to Chickerell was on 16th August 1935 (following on from one held at Swanage the previous day), with the *Echo* on this occasion describing the venue as 'Chickerell Racecourse' rather than 'Chickerell Aerodrome' as it had always done previously. There were two shows, one at 2.30 in the afternoon, the other four hours later. Once more the local newspaper gave away free flight tickets to its readers.

The show opened with a mass flypast of the whole aircraft fleet, led by Sir Alan's Chief Pilot – Flight Lieutenant Hugh C. Johnson, who had amassed by that time a total number of passengers safely carried of over 150,000!

Whilst the show was similar to that in previous years, one new display was formation aerobatics by three aircraft joined together at their wing tips by ribbons. Another was a parachute descent – by Miss

Naomi Heron-Maxwell – using a static line for a 'pull-off' from the lower wing of one of the biplanes.

Local area passenger flights were actually cheaper than in 1932, costing 4/- (20p), but with ground admission being priced at 1/3d (6½p) for adults and 6d (2½p) for children and – a sign of the times – a car parking fee of 1/- (5p) also being charged. Was this the start of the high priced parking which brings the town so much criticism today?

Flights with 'famous pilots', as well as the local area flights, were also offered for as little as 4/- (20p), but it was jokingly said that on some occasions the flights were so short that the undercarriage mains wheels were still rotating from the take-off run when the aircraft landing run commenced!

Despite such minor niggles, it is worth noting that prior to Sir Alan Cobham's shows ending in 1935, some three million people paid to see the events, an equally large number watched them free of charge from nearby vantage points, and over a million brave souls made their first flight in the hands of the great man's barn-storming pilots!

Sir Alan also promoted aviation by becoming involved with the silver screen, the film "The King's Cup" being a thrilling romance of the air based upon a story that he wrote and starred Dorothy Bouchier and Harry Milton. In it the thrills of aviation are allied to a romantic drama and a keenly contested race for an important air race trophy, with one vivid scene portraying aircraft flying below the levels of the Mendip Hills around Cheddar Gorge. Its first local screening was at the Plaza Cinema in Dorchester in August 1933.

So, even if Sir Alan failed in his overall aim of promoting aviation to the greater awareness that he felt it warranted, he certainly brought it to the attention of 'the man in the street'.

His later achievements included the successful innovation of air-to-air refuelling techniques. He died in 1973, and is buried at Tarrant Rushton. But his strong connection with Chickerell is commemorated by the name of the main street on the housing side of the development that covers the aerodrome: 'Cobham Drive'.

Gliding at Bincombe
The Dorset Gliding Club is still in existence and very active, and – after a series of enforced changes of gliding sites – now operates from Gallows Hill, near to The Royal Armoured Corps Centre at Bovington

The Alpha Flying Services Spartan Three-Seater Mk 1 G-ABLJ on the ground at Lodmoor in the summer of 1933. Houses at Overcombe Corner can be seen behind the tail, with the road to Bowleaze Cove climbing over the hill beyond.

Camp.

On an August evening in 1933 the club held a meeting at Bincombe, north of Weymouth on Ridgeway Hill and embarked on some ridge soaring – that is to say 'riding' the vertical air currents generated on the side of a hill when the wind blows across it at an angle of about ninety degrees.

Watched by hundreds of holidaymakers, the Club's glider *Dorsling* took off into a southerly wind of some 25 to 35 mph and managed to stay airborne for 35 minutes, beating the previous Club record of 20 minutes which had been set on an earlier occasion in the skies above Weymouth's White Horse chalk hill-carving of George III. Contemporary reports state 'Such was the force of the wind, that when the machine landed it came to the ground almost vertically.'

A Young Lady
The Alpha Flying Services pilot working out of Lodmoor was involved that same summer of 1933 in a story rather like the plot of an old movie.

Just before 4.00 in the afternoon on 23rd August a lady arrived at the airstrip and approached the AFS manager Mr A.F. Willys in a state of some anxiety after arriving at Weymouth by steamer from the Channel Islands. She wished to charter an aircraft to try and get her to Plymouth where the liner *Manhattan* was due to call for mails before setting heading for Le Havre at 5.45 pm, and where the young lady was due to meet her fiancé.

Frustrated by 30 mph headwinds, the pilot,

Captain Davies (a former RFC, then RAF pilot), just failed to meet the deadline, for the liner had sailed and was to be seen just outside the harbour breakwater – where the seas were too rough for any fast local ship to give chase. Davies returned to Lodmoor with his fare where, because the aircraft was not fitted for night flying, Mr Willys arranged for a car to take the love-lorn young woman to Southampton to await the next available vessel to Le Havre and her North Atlantic crossing. I wonder if so much effort would have been expended if the stranded passenger had been one bereft of pretty face and slender figure?

After a couple of changes in ownership, G-ABLJ saw out her days as a training aid for air cadets, having been donated to The Air Training Corps in 1944.

Two Royal Visits

An earlier incident of interest that 1933 summer was centred not at Lodmoor, but on Chickerell. On Thursday 13th July HRH The Prince of Wales – later King Edward VIII – was due to fly to Weymouth from London to officially open the Weymouth Harbour Reconstruction Scheme.

The day dawned with the local area subjected to dense drizzle and a low cloud base – but there was not enough time for the Prince to get to Dorset by rail to make his planned arrival time of 12.30 pm, so flown by his personal pilot Captain E.H. Fielden, he set off in his distinctive blue and red DH 84 Dragon biplane to attempt the journey. By the time they had reached the Swanage the weather had become so poor that it was considered too dangerous to continue, and Captain Fielden – after circling the area for some ten minutes – elected to land in a field at Gorlestone. The Prince continued his journey in the car of Captain F.H. Bacon, director of the Swanage Tile & Brick Co, who had watched the twin-engined aircraft's unscheduled arrival.

Meanwhile at Chickerell the large crowd, including over 2,000 local children who had planned to greet the royal arrival with a display which, from the air, would represent the Prince of Wales' feathers became excited as exactly at 12.30 a monoplane appeared from the low cloud and landed in front of them. It was not, of course, the Prince, but the press photographers who had flown in to cover the occasion!

A little later, back in the town, the Prince was seen to have thick mud on his shoes and trouser turn-ups as he entered the Gloucester Hotel – itself a former royal residence – for lunch prior to the ceremonies at harbour side!

The Prince's father, King George V, had returned to Weymouth the previous July. As on his 1912 visit twenty years earlier, he once more came to review the Home Fleet. There was again major aviation involvement – but on this occasion it was the airfield at Chickerell, rather than that at Lodmoor, which was the centre of activity, with numerous RAF and private aircraft in evidence.

Noting this flurry of aeronautical action, and recognising the geographically central location of Weymouth on any air route between the important ports of Portsmouth, Southampton and Plymouth, the Town Council considered that same month the formal establishment of a licensed airfield at Chickerell, acknowledging that it would have to reach a compromise with The Electricity Commission about the routing of National Grid power cables, but decided 'that no action be taken on the matter'.

Later in the month the Weymouth Chamber of Commerce wrote to the Council stating its conviction that 'that an Air Port for Weymouth and the district is of the greatest importance, and the provision is essential if Weymouth is to hold its place with other south coast ports in the future. We therefore respectfully urge the Town Council to reconsider their decision not to proceed with the acquisition of the proposed site at Chickerell, and to take whatever steps are necessary to secure the land, which we understand is the only suitable land which could be scheduled as an A1 Port'.

The Council was not swayed by the argument and re-stated its decision 'that no action be taken on the matter'. In October of the following year a further attempt was made to obtain a local licensed aerodrome, when two councillors moved a Notice of Motion arguing that in the interests of the Borough as a health resort and pleasure resort, and also commercially, it was essential that an airport be established. As on previous occasions, the Motion was defeated.

The M2 Tragedy

It was also in 1932 that a tragedy occurred with a local aviation connection of a different kind, when the submarine M2 sank in West Bay – not too far from the Chesil Beach Bombing Range, an area which we shall look at in some detail later.

M2 underway on the surface, showing clearly the Peto aircraft, the hangar and the launching & recovery crane. On the extreme left of the picture, can be seen one of the two RAF mechanics serving aboard.

The mammoth submarine was formally a K Class vessel (K19) and, pre-conversion in 1927 to an aircraft carrier submarine, was fitted with a single 12" gun. Now fitted with a hangar where the gun armament had originally been, she was equipped to carry a small Parnall Peto floatplane (serial number N255), a two crew reconnaissance aircraft with a range of just over 200 miles and a top speed of 98 knots.

On the morning of 26th January she was seen to dive in her allotted exercise area, but it was not until dusk, when she failed to report in on the radio or return to port, that it was realised that something was amiss. Although unresolved beyond all reasonable doubt, it seems that the hangar doors became open underwater carrying the M2 to her death with the loss of all 6 officers, 47 ratings and 2 RAF airmen aboard.

Joining the surface units involved in the hunt for survivors of the submarine were Supermarine Southampton flying boats of No 201 Squadron, an early example of fixed-wing search and rescue operations.

Four years later, in 1936, the first Short 'C' Class flying boat – Canopus – took to the skies, the prototype flying boat of a class designed to operate the 'Empire Air Route'. On occasions, these large machines were seen above Weymouth – presumably on route proving flights (the seaplane airport in Poole Harbour was nearby) or to give publicity to the innovative aircraft.

The British Hospitals Air Pageant

To return to happier events, the year after the loss of the M2, on 11th July 1933, another aeronautical extravaganza took place at Chickerell, when the aircraft of The British Hospitals Air Pageant, with Captain Charles Scott AFC – then the holder of the England to Australia speed record – as Chief Pilot and with fifteen other pilots in attendance, operated from the airstrip, having been beaten by the weather at Dorchester the previous Friday when no passengers were carried.

Once again the *Dorset Daily Echo* had offered free flights to its readers, those missing out on the Dorchester event (which was to have been held at Middle Farm – now the site of the Poundbury village) being offered the chance to fly from Chickerell. Up to fifteen aircraft participated in the pageant, the proceeds from which were to go to the Dorset County Hospital, with one of the winners, SRN Sister Jarrard, being taken up for her flight before the programme officially commenced, as she had to get to work to attend to her patients. Another lucky winner, a veteran of the First World War, proffered the comment that he would 'sooner go up in a plane than ride on the pillion of a motorcycle'.

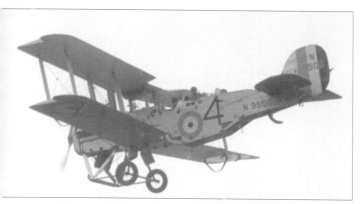

Westland Walrus N9500 of the type operated at Chickerell by No 420 Flight of the Fleet Air Arm. Note the Scarf Ring fitting in the rear cockpit for the mounting of a Lewis Gun. (This aircraft should not be confused with the much better know Walrus amphibian of air sea rescue fame during the Second World War .)

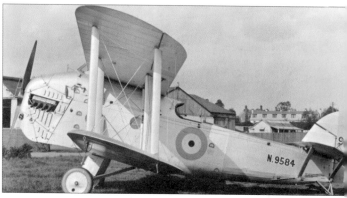

Blackburn Blackburn R Mk 1 N9584; not of 420 Flt, nor on the ground at Chickerell - but posing after factory roll-out for a Blackburn Aircraft Ltd publicity shot. Contemporary of the better known Avro Bison fleet reconnaissance biplane, the Blackburn boasted a similar 'chunky' engine shape and deep fuselage.

With reference to Dorchester, it is worth mentioning that Middle Farm was the site of a short-lived airfield, additional to the two at Weymouth. It was in use from March 1934, and was an 'on request' landing site on Provincial Airways route from Plymouth to Croydon using single-engined de Havilland DH83 Fox Moth aircraft, which could carry four passengers.

The short runway was very limiting and demanding upon the pilots, and the site was apparently abandoned only three months later after one of the Fox Moth aircraft crashed on take-off on 25th June, thereby highlighting the field's inadequacies! The aircraft, flown by Captain S.W.A. Scott, had landed safely after its flight from Plymouth, with a single passenger. On take-off for Croydon with an additional two people on board, including Peter Hanbury son of the North Dorset MP Cecil Hanbury, it failed to clear standing crops on the edge of the flying area and ended up on its nose some half a mile from Maiden Castle. Nobody was seriously injured, but extensive damage was done to the Fox Moth, the registration of which was G-ACCF. (This was a bad week for Provincial Airways, for on the 19th June another of its Fox Moths, G-ACEX captained by E Ellison, had also ended up on its nose at a south coast airfield – this time at Ashley, near Lymington in Hampshire. Again, nobody was seriously hurt).

The following year the Dorset County Council approached the Duchy of Cornwall – large local landowners – seeking a site for a permanent airfield for the county town of Dorchester, but the Duchy

was unable to offer anywhere suitable and the project then seems quietly to have been dropped.

Chickerell Flying Ground between the Wars

Militarily in the 1920s, Chickerell was used, mainly in the summer months, by aircraft exercising with Portland-based naval vessels. Units visiting included the FAA's No 420 (Fleet Spotter) Flight, with its Westland Walrus three-seat reconnaissance biplanes – not to be confused with the Supermarine Walrus amphibians of later years – and, later, Blackburn TSR Mk 1s, and No 447 (Fleet Spotter) Flight, which flew Fairey IIIF aircraft. For example, in April 1929 a IIIF of 447 Flt spotted off Portland for a shoot by the 13.5" gun, 35,000 ton battle cruiser HMS *Tiger*. Until 1st April 1924 both of the flights had been RAF units; each ceased to exist in 1929, being disbanded to become No 449 and No 421 Flights embarked on HMS *Furious*.

The support facilities at Chickerell in these days were minimal: just a windsock, white landing circle and a few tents. On a non-aviation front, it might be noted that it was in the 1930s that parts of the aerodrome first started to be used as municipal playing fields.

On the morning of 23rd June 1924, and initially unknown to the pilot, one of 420 Flt's Westland Walrus aircraft, serial number N9512, damaged its undercarriage on taking-off from Chickerell. The efforts of the pilot of another aircraft with which it was in formation to draw N9512's crew attention to its predicament were in vain, so the aircraft's

With engine bay and fuselage almost completely submerged, Westland Walrus N9512 of 420 Flt, FAA, is towed ashore after being ditched off Weymouth Beach on 23rd June 1924.

telegraphist was contacted by wireless telephony and the crew instructed not to land back at Chickerell, but to proceed to Weymouth Bay and carry out a controlled ditching close inshore.

The pilot, Pilot Officer Beilby, brought the biplane down some 200 yards out from the beach, but the nose dipped under the surface of the sea before the small flotilla of launches rushing to the rescue reached it, and a race against time and tide ensued. The local vessels *Laurel*, *Southern Maid* and *Weymouth Belle* were joined by a pinnace from the 15"gun, 37,000 ton battleship *HMS Queen Elizabeth*, which was in the local area participating in the celebrations to mark the 30th birthday of the Prince of Wales.

Supported by a Board of Trade vessel from Portland, which had come to the scene, the Walrus was towed ashore at Greenhill – where a Flt Lt Malet had arrived from Chickerell to take charge of the recovery, under the eyes of literally hundreds of onlookers. Plt Off Beilby was slightly injured in the ditching, but the observer, Lt Wilson, and Telegraphist Morsley were unscathed.

The ditching was successful in that the crew were saved, but when the aircraft was salvaged it was classified as 'beyond economic repair'.

Weymouth's lack of a proper aerodrome was highlighted on the night of 11th/12th July 1936, when a Mr Samuels, the civilian pilot of an aircraft chartered from Surrey Flying Services, was taken ill at 7,000 feet above Portland Harbour whilst acting as a target for the Territorial Army. Assisted by the ground engineer and two wireless operators on board, Samuels was forced to fly all the way back to Southampton, where he collapsed after landing.

There was a contingency plan for the aircraft to land on Weymouth Sands in a dire emergency, with the police and fire brigade to have been alerted by the TA unit that it was exercising with, but the pilot elected to try for a more conventional return to Mother Earth. His condition rapidly improved and although he was not admitted to hospital it was felt prudent to accommodate him at Southampton Airport overnight. 'Had there been an aerodrome at Weymouth', Major R M Dawes of the Royal Engineers commented, 'Everything would have been alright'.

The Chesil Bank Bombing Ranges

With war in Europe becoming daily more likely, and Britain's armed forces scrambling to regain some semblance of their former fighting prowess, the Air Ministry in 1935 embarked upon a search for nine coastal bombing and gunnery ranges. It was only able to identify six suitable sites – one of which was in Lyme Bay off the Chesil Bank. (Lyme Bay is often referred to locally as West Bay, and I have used both terms in this book.)

The Bay was already in use by the Royal Navy as a training area for general naval training, anti-submarine warfare training and most especially for training in the skills of minesweeping. In these pre-radar days, the Admiralty was particularly concerned that any range marker buoys sited as

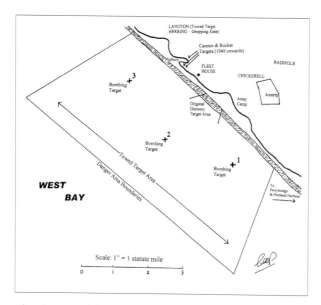

Sketch map of the Chesil Bank Bombing Ranges.

requested by the Air Ministry would constitute a major hazard to military shipping.

In a dummy run on the range, or maybe exercising 'clear range' procedures, a seaplane was reported as carrying out machine gun firing practice just 500 yards off the beach on 15th January 1935. A 'clear range' procedure is one where practice firing or bombing can be carried after the aircraft crew itself has ascertained that the target area is clear of shipping.

After extensive initial reservations, the Senior Naval Officer, Portland, agreed to the ranges being established, but only provided they were 'entirely under Naval control'. Completely different reservations, about the effect of the ranges on the wildlife of the area, particularly the Mute Swan population in the Abbotsbury area and the rare underwater weed *Zostera Nana*, were widely aired, with the Earl of Crawford using a debate in the House of Lords in December 1935 to raise strong objections. In rather less glamorous forums, Portland Urban District Council, on 10th April, and Chickerell Parish Council, at a special meeting on 2nd May, also formally recorded their own objections to the proposals.

Letters flew to and forth between the Admiralty and the Air Ministry until an uneasy compromise was finally reached:

1. The seaward marker buoys (subject to Board of Trade approval) would not be laid.
2. The total area to be kept clear of shipping would be reduced from the area proposed in the original plans, and the 'Central Range Area' for air firing would be abandoned.
3. HM ships would stay clear of the new range area whenever possible.
4. Bombing and gunnery activity would cease when ships did have to enter the area.
5. There would be an interchange of training programmes between the staffs of the Captain-in-Charge, Portland and of the Air Officer Commanding whichever RAF Bomber Command Group Headquarters was to be responsible for the running of the ranges.
6. Fleet Air Arm (FAA) requirements to use the range would be fully met.

It was not only on the naval front that objections to the plans for the ranges were raised. When the Air Ministry advised Weymouth Corporation (who owned the land, despite it being physically located within the parish of Chickerell, and was already debating its future) that it intended to acquire the former 'Chickerell Flying Ground' as a support base for the new ranges, many objections were raised which, with the passage of time and the benefit of hindsight, seem short sighted when ominous signs of war were almost daily making themselves seen and heard on continental Europe.

Some councillors feared that the siting of an airfield at Chickerell would make Weymouth a prime military target if hostilities did break out. Others felt that the upgrading of the flying field could only be beneficial to the town as internal and international air services expanded – whilst the concern of others seemed only to be associated with the loss of the Municipal Playing Fields!

In the end, after the Air Ministry said that it would resort to using its compulsory purchase powers if necessary, a compromise was reached and the land passed into Air Ministry ownership for £7,500, but with some 10 acres being kept available as playing fields provided no structures were erected which could interfere with flying operations. The financial aspects of the deal negotiated were to favour the Council some twenty or so years later, when it was able to buy the land back at the same price that it had received for it – a reflection of the financial negotiating skills of the Town Clerks: Mr Percy Smallman at the time of selling and Mr Jack Jones at the time of buying back.

So on 1st September 1937, just one month later than planned for, the ranges opened, with peace time restrictions being imposed to ban all firing or bombing between 6.00 pm on a Saturday until 6.00

am on a Monday.

Indicative of the urgent need to re-arm and re-train was the fact that, by special Board of Trade dispensation, the range byelaws were not promulgated until some time after the official opening.

As war grew imminent, a team from Dundee came to the area in the summer of 1939 to install floodlighting, in the form of illuminated arrows, on the beach targets. Cables were laid across The Fleet, the brackish, semi-tidal stretch of shallow water between the mainland and the pebble bank, from an electrical sub-station near Fleet Manor. The lights were non-operational at the outbreak of war due to blackout restrictions and were not used until much later on.

Typical of the squadrons using the ranges in those early days was No 500 Squadron, whose 'B' Flight Avro Anson maritime patrol aircraft, under the command of Fg Off P Green, were detached to RAF Warmwell from their home base at Detling, in Kent, during August 1939 – only days before the outbreak of war.

The wartime ARP 'Bomb Plot' map of the former Borough of Weymouth and Melcombe Regis – which is still in existence and on display at Weymouth's Brewer's Quay Museum – shows that during hostilities two sticks of HE bombs dropped in the vicinity of the Chickerell airfield: 5 bombs to the south and 4 along the northern boundary. No record exists of any actual damage caused, if any, to the RAF facilities. (Weymouth was one of the most heavily bombed towns, relative to its size, in the country: 4,300 incendiary, 481 high explosive, 9 oil and 4 land mine bombs dropped on the borough during the war years.)

The Lyme Regis Air Sea Rescue Unit

To provide support facilities for the Chesil Bank Bombing Ranges, No 37 Air Sea Rescue and Marine Craft Unit (ASRMCU) was formed at Lyme Regis in 1937, with the Air Sea Rescue aspect being very much a secondary task until the outbreak of the war.

The range safety duties included being on patrol in the area should an accident occur to an aircraft using the ranges and also to provide moving targets in addition to the moored targets off the Chesil Bank itself. This latter duty was provided in two ways: a conventional towed-target pulled behind one of the RSLs (range safety launches) and an armoured target vessel [A565] at which practice bombs were actually

Aerial post war view of the Ranges, showing one of the bomb plotting and observation facilities atop the beach.

The view is taken looking along Chesil Bank towards Portland, with the open sea to the right and The Fleet, with one of its landing jetties, on the left.

aimed (but which could also tow a conventional target).

The armoured target boat was fitted with three 1,000 hp Napier Lion engines and constructed with a triple skinned mahogany hull, cased extensively above the waterline with armour plate. It was equipped with a 'dead man's handle' type of device which throttled back the engines, in the case of a direct hit rendering the crew concussed or incapable, and a gyro override which applied deflection to the rudders to put the craft into a circular path until the crew regained control or the designated safety vessel ('The Chaser') could come alongside.

The crew of A565 received 1/- (5p) per day safety money – and as much fish as they could recover after the bombing runs were completed! Often the catch was sufficient for some to be sent across to RAF Warmwell to supplement the ASRMCU's parenting unit's food supplies. The armoured boat left the unit on 29th December 1944.

In addition to supporting the range activities of the front line squadrons, the unit was also called upon to assist at a variety of trials conducted by Boscombe Down, Farnborough and Porton Down – this last unit, for example, conducting what the Operations Record Book called 'smoke trials' in the late autumn of 1943.

No 37 Air Sea Rescue and Marine Craft Unit is credited with the saving of 65 lives during the Second World War. The unit stayed operational until July 1964 (outlasting the bombing ranges in their original form), parenting responsibility initially being taken over by RAF Exeter when RAF Warmwell closed down soon after the cessation of hostilities.

From 1959 the main tasking was Search & Rescue standby, but even this gradually took on less and less importance as the operational flexibility of rapidly improving helicopters and their winching equipment and techniques moved to the fore.

For some ten years after the closure of the RAF unit at Lyme Regis, two local fishing craft were contracted to the Ministry of Defence as range safety vessels, their tasking being to keep the ranges clear of other craft when live exercises were taking place, to be on hand in case of accidents and to recover non-explosive stores dropped from, mainly, trials aircraft.

It was, throughout the RAF, the success of the Search & Rescue helicopter force which led to the demise of the UK Air Sea Rescue and Marine Craft Units. The Marine Craft Units left in the United Kingdom, which are civilian manned, are involved solely in the provision of target towing facilities to aircraft such as Nimrods and Tornadoes, employed in the maritime attack role, and in the training of Search & Rescue helicopter crews.

The 1938 Fleet Review

If the 1912 Royal Naval Review off Weymouth and Portland sent the scene locally for the hostilities of the 1914 – 1918 Great War, so did a very similar pageant in 1938 in respect of the Second World War.

At 6.30 pm on the evening of 20th June, HM King George VI – with the Duke of Kent accompanying him as his Aide de Campe – arrived at Weymouth Railway Station to review his fleet. Almost 80 warships awaited their sovereign, who led them to an exercise area some 20 miles south west of Portland Bill the following morning.

At this time the orthodox naval thinking was that the battleship still ruled the waves, but activity during their time at sea showed that there was a definite acceptance that aircraft did have an increasing role to play in maritime warfare. His Majesty's party – aboard HMS Nelson – was to see an appreciable amount of aviation activity during the day.

In addition to viewing the flying-off of three Walrus scout aircraft from their mother cruisers in the 2nd Cruiser Division to operate in the gun-spotting role, the King was as impressed as those around him when ships' anti-aircraft fire downed a Queen Bee target biplane – the de Haviland Queen Bee aircraft being a radio-controlled, unmanned

variant of the Tiger Moth trainer. Hit by a shell from a high angle 4" anti-aircraft gun, the £2,000 drone fell into the sea from some 10,000 feet.

A second Queen Bee was engaged at low level by the 8 barrel, 40 mm Pom Pom guns, but bore a charmed life and escaped unscathed – possibly because the guns were actually firing in an offset (practice) mode.

Perhaps, though, the most impressive sight was a co-ordinated mock attack upon the fleet by 24 Supermarine Swordfish aircraft from the carrier HMS Courageous – 18 in the torpedo-carrying role and the other 6 as dive-bombers – these latter aircraft bombing a 'splash target' being towed astern of one of the warships at some 18 knots.

The next day, the exercise concluded, the King returned to London by rail but, always an aviation enthusiast, the Duke of Kent returned to the capital by air from Warmwell – still known until the following month as RAF Woodsford.

Sadly, two of the main characters from this interlude were soon to be no more. HMS Courageous was sunk with heavy loss of life by U-29 on 17th September 1939 – the Royal Navy's first capital ship loss in the Second World War (and one of five RN carriers to be sunk by German U-boats). The Duke of Kent was killed in the crash of Sunderland W4026/M of 228 Sqn in Caithness on 25th August 1942, whilst en route to Iceland.

I am ending this chapter on the inter-war years with this postcard listing the names of those lost in the sinking of the M2 – a reminder that, even in peacetime, our servicemen and women risk their lives in the service of our country. (The skew of the writing is, by the way, as the memento was printed.)

THREE

The Second World War

Lysanders at Chickerell

During the early summer of 1940, just as the Battle of Britain was about to start and change the course of history, the FAA's No 793 Squadron, based at RNAS Ford in Sussex, used the Chickerell facilities whilst its Blackburn Roc Mk 1 target-towing aircraft were detached to RAF Warmwell.

From before and until after their departure, continued use was made of the airstrip in the tension-filled spring and early summer of 1940. Westland Lysander aircraft and personnel of 'B' Flight of No 613 (City of Manchester) Squadron were detached to Chickerell on 22nd April from their home-base at RAF Odiham in Hampshire –tasked to fly anti-invasion patrols off the Dorset coastline.

Five pilots, under the command of Sqn Ldr P W Stansfield, were detached, at least two of whom, sadly, did not survive the war. Plt Off Hugh Gore, was shot down and killed in 1943 whilst flying a 613 Sqn Mustang Mk1, and Plt Off Sandy Webb, by then a Wing Commander, was shot down in 1945 whilst leading a wing of Tempests.

Another, Paddy Barthropp, left the squadron in the summer of 1940 when volunteers were called for the Battle of Britain. He was shot down three times, awarded the Distinguished Flying Cross and ended up as a prisoner of war in Stalag Luft III. Post-war he rose to the rank of Wing Commander, was awarded the Air Force Cross, and is now Life President of the No 613 Squadron Association.

(The squadron wasn't fully converted to an all Lysander unit until June 1940, when it gave up the last of its ageing Hawker Hector aircraft. 613 Sqn later graduated to the more formidable Tomahawk and, later, to Mustang aircraft.)

One of the wooden huts at Chickerell was used as an Operations and Briefing room, whilst many of the personnel were accommodated off-base, including the officers who enjoyed the hospitality of the nearby Alexandra Inn.

By road, rail and air, the detachment returned to RAF Odiham on 13th May 1940 and, as the threat of Nazi invasion increased following the Dunkirk evacuation, the airstrip was then blocked off as a

Above The pilots of 613 Sqn who operated out of Chickerell in 1940 pose, on a pleasant April day, outside their temporary 'B' Flight Headquarters – complete with the 'mandatory' squadron mascot!

Back row (left to right): Plt Offs Sandy Webb and J.C. Paterson; front row (left to right): Plt Off Paddy Barthropp, Sqn Ldr P.W. Stansfield and Plt Off Hugh Gore.

Below Two of the 613 Sqn pilots outside their 'home' at Chickerell in April and May 1940: Plt Offs Hugh Gore (left) and Sandy Webb. Sadly, both were later shot down in action and killed.

'Bomb Gone!'. With Chesil Beach clearly visible in the background, Wellington BJ895 flies on a southerly heading down the Fleet as the spherical weapon drops away before hitting the surface and commencing its bouncing trajectory across the water.

All ranks Christmas lunch at Chickerell in 1941. Although the majority of the personnel appear to be from the Army, a few RAF uniforms can be picked out.

potential landing ground by having a number of old cars strategically placed upon it. The ranges were also temporarily closed down – to be opened again in October when the military situation had sufficiently improved.

Lysander aircraft were back in the Weymouth area again in May 1941, when aircraft of Odiham's No 225 Squadron flew south from their detached base at Tilshead on Salisbury Plain to participate in a major anti-invasion exercise held locally, although by now – unknown at the time of course – Hitler's attention was almost exclusively drawn eastwards and Operation Sea Lion had been indefinitely postponed. 225 Sqn had the previous year been flying patrols of a similar nature to 613's along the coastlines of Hampshire and the Isle of Wight and, like its sister squadron, later went on to fly Mustang aircraft in the tactical reconnaissance role.

During the winter months of 1941/1942 a Royal Artillery anti-aircraft radar unit was stationed at Chickerell, with the soldiers sharing the facilities of their colleagues in light blue.

Barnes Wallis and the 'Bouncing Bomb'

Perhaps the Chesil Bank Bombing Ranges' greatest claim to fame during both the war years was its involvement in the development trials of the Barnes Wallis 'Upkeep' and 'Highball' bouncing bombs.

The 'Upkeep' weapon was the one that went on to successful use in Operation Chastise, the Dam Buster Raids on the night of 16th/17th May 1943 by No 617 Squadron, but the 'Highball' anti-shipping weapon was never used in anger. It was not ready for operational use until 1944, by which time the enemy's naval surface shipping force (as opposed to its submarine force) was rapidly becoming marginalised. There may also have been a fear that the Germans might copy it and make use of it against naval allied vessels which, in contrast, were still major players in the war. No 618 Squadron eventually deployed to the Far East with Highball, for anticipated use against the Japanese Navy – but events at Hiroshima and Nagasaki dictated otherwise.

Late in 1942 a Mark III Wellington bomber – serial number BJ895 – had been modified at the Vickers' factory to carry two small scale 'Golf Mine' bombs, and it was these 46" diameter trial bombs, which were mounted in the Wellington's bomb bay and given back spin by a chain drive from a motor mounted within the aircraft, that were dropped at Chesil Bank, the actual target area normally being the waters of The Fleet. The actual Upkeep bombs were not significant only in their shape and the spin applied to them; they were also the largest bombs in RAF service at that time – and remained so until

The remains of one of the two trial spherical bombs, which were recovered from the Fleet in September 1973. One initially went to Weymouth Museum, and was displayed at its sister Portland Museum; the other went to the RAF Museum at Henlow. Apparently, a further trial bomb was recovered in 1992.

Tallboy and, later, Grand Slam bombs (both Wallis designs) became operational. Their weights were 9,250lb (4,200kg), 12,000lb (5,448kg) and a massive 22,000lb (9,988kg) respectively.

The first trial took place on 4th December 1942, BJ895 flying directly to the ranges from Weybridge, with Captain J. 'Mutt' Summers (the test pilot who did the very first flight in the prototype Spitfire) at the controls, and with both weapons being dropped from an altitude of 200' in the West Fleet – probably somewhere between Langton Herring and Abbotsbury. Wallis flew on this mission as bomb aimer. Although much useful data was gathered, the trial was not a success, as both spheres broke up on impact with the water.

Strengthening of the trial bombs, followed by a period of bad weather, delayed the next flight until 15th December, with the bomber this time taking off from RAF Warmwell and carrying two slightly different spheres – one with a smooth outer surface and the other with a dimpled one. Neither drop was considered a success, but Wallis was able to retrieve one of the weapons, which was badly damaged but, to his relief, had not actually shattered on impact.

Christmas modifications to the spheres, and winter weather, delayed the next flight until 9th January 1943, after which further flights were conducted – with varying degrees of success – until a perfect '13 bounces' drop was achieved off Langton Hive Point on 23rd January, with an even more impressive '20 – 22 bounces' drop being realised the next day. Four more trial flights took place in February and a final set on 8th March, these latter drops being carried out to seaward of the Chesil Bank.

On display at the Abbotsbury Swannery today can be seen one of the inert 'dimpled' spherical trial bombs, which was recovered from the Fleet on 30th September 1992 – in a joint operation involving a team from the British Museum and the Royal Navy [who provided a Sea King helicopter for the lifting of the trial weapon from the seabed].

All the Chesil Bank trials had been conducted with the scaled-down 'Golf Mine' spherical weapons, from the modified Wellington. On 13th April trials of the full size weapons commenced at Reculver, Kent, using full size weapons and Lancaster, Mosquito and still, occasionally, Wellington aircraft. A great wartime moral booster was imminent!

Aerial view from an aeroplane manoeuvring above the Abbotsbury Swannery end of the beach, with Chesil Beach itself clearly visible and the Isle of Portland dominating the skyline beyond. The majority of the local bouncing bomb trials took place in the narrow waterway between the mainland and the beach.

Target-towing

In the spring of 1943 a second FAA target-towing unit was detached to Warmwell from RNAS Yeovilton, *HMS Heron*, and made visits to Chickerell: No 794 Squadron, which was equipped with Blackburn Rocs, Boulton Paul Defiant TT IIIs, and Miles Masters and Martinets. As the longest landing and take-off distance available at Chickerell was just 2,400 feet (731m), the airfield was restricted to aircraft no larger than of Blenheim or Hampden size. Smaller aeroplanes such as these target facilities aircraft were using the strip exactly as it was designed to be used: to re-fuel and re-arm whilst operating on the ranges, and as a 'bolt hole' in the case of an in-flight emergency.

When air-to-air firing practice was taking place, it was the custom for the bullets to be colour-coded in the following manner: each pilot or air gunner's ammunition would have a different colour painted at the tip of each round, and as the rounds penetrated the towed-target banner their passage would leave a coloured mark corresponding to the colour of the bullet tip – so it was possible to assess how many hits each of the aircraft had made. To save the transit time of the target aircraft returning to Warmwell, or even to Chickerell, a banner dropping zone was established north west of the Chickerell airstrip to the south of Tatton House, on land which now forms

Above Boulton Paul Defiant target tug aircraft T4007, of No 794 Squadron of the Fleet Air Arm – but taken in 1944 at RNAS St Merryn, Cornwall, and not earlier at Chickerell. Note that a winch operator's position now occupies that once taken up by the 4x.303" gun turret fitted to the aircraft in the fighter role.

The Blackburn Rocs which flew out of Chickerell with 794 Sqn, were a similar aircraft – again with the gun turret removed.

Below Another 794 Sqn aircraft – this time a Miles Master TT MkII, W9026, portrayed at RNAS Dale, in south west Wales, in 1941.

part of Dingle Dell Moor Farm, and it was here that the initial scoring often took place. Although not designed as a flying field, it was not unknown for the occasional aircraft to land there.

Rockets on the Ranges

As the Allies' emphasis turned from defence to attack, aircraft such as 'Hurri-bombers' dropped practice bombs on the seaborne targets. In the run up to the D-Day landings, ground attack aircraft such as the Typhoon could regularly be seen carrying out practice rocket attacks on the ranges – most especially at the targets set atop the beach opposite the old Coastguard Cottages at Clouds Hill, (between Langton Herring and the Swannery, and not to be confused with the site of Lawrence of Arabia's cottage inland on Bovington Heath).

In the nature of things such as high speed, low level flying, errors inevitably occurred – such as the day when one Typhoon pilot managed to put his rockets through one of the cottages! On another occasion a Me109 pilot is reputed to have mistaken one of the moored targets as a 'target of opportunity'

Tug airborne over an unwelcoming sea, but not Lyme Bay! Here we see a Miles Martinet TT Mk1, bearing the unit markings T8K and operated by 771 Sqn out of RNAS Twatt in the Orkney Islands. The target drogue is 'close hauled' to the aircraft and appears to have been severely mauled by gunfire. It will be dropped alongside the runway, or at an alternative designated dropping zone, before the aircraft lands.

and opened fire on it – possibly the only range target to be used by both sides during the whole conflict?

The activities of the larger bomber and maritime patrol aircraft continued, with free-fall bombing being scored by triangulation from three blockhouses located in the general area of Wyke Regis, Chickerell and Langton Herring. One bonus to the local military units continued to be the gathering-in of fish killed by the blast of the practice bombs!

FOUR

The Post-War Years

The Ranges stay open

With the cessation of hostilities in Europe and then in the Far East, the RAF went into a rapid 'scale down'. Although RAF Warmwell and its resident Armament Practice Camps closed down even before 1945 had drawn to a close, the ranges were one place not selected for disestablishment – a fact far from popular with the local fishing community. In 1948 the Southern Fisheries Committee formally objected to the retention of the ranges, stating that its use seriously interfered with the activities of some 20 to 30 seine net fishing boats. However, a sensible dialogue between the military and the fishermen produced a satisfactory compromise and the Ministry of Agriculture was happy to accept this state of affairs. At the same time some half-hearted objections were raised about the continuing use of the Army's small arms range at Chickerell Army Camp, where the safety zone extended towards Chesil Bank, but these came to nothing.

With 'Peace in Our Time' still not assured, for the Cold War was now very much a fact of life, the facilities provided in 1949 were:

1. Three practice bombing targets (wooden, painted yellow and with pole and basket identifiers), and on

Built during the war years, the accommodation huts at Chickerell continued in use until the unit's closure. The Boiler Room is to the right, with the cooks 'whites' out to dry nearby.

Vertical picture of the airfield at Chickerell taken by an RAF Photo Reconnaissance aircraft in August 1947.

The airstrip lies immediately above the inverted triangle of land near the centre of the frame, with the domestic and technical buildings and dark-roofed hangar clearly visible alongside Radipole Lane.

Note, to the north east, the bunkers on Weymouth Golf Course.

A photograph taken in 1951 from a navigation training Vickers Wellington aircraft, showed little change at Chickerell in the intervening 4 years

which only small smoke ('puff') bombs could be dropped.

2. One live rocket projectile firing range, for use only during daylight hours.

3. One combined air-to-ground gunnery (maximum calibre 20 mm) and inert rocket projectile firing range.

It was proposed to erect two new quadrant shelters, two dive screens and one marker shelter. It was from the quadrant buildings that the bombing accuracy was assessed. Bearings were taken from a minimum of two of them and passed by landline to the Range Control Tower, from whence the bombing results were passed to the aircraft by radio. Earlier the radio operator would have passed to aircraft arriving at the range the local sea level atmospheric pressure (known as 'The QNH' and used as the aircraft's altimeter setting datum), co-ordinated the height from which the aircraft was to operate and, of course, passed other safety data and given permission, or otherwise, to commence bombing or gun-firing.

At this time the Air Ministry owned 52 acres of land (Chickerell airfield), with 383 acres on lease from the original agreement and a further 24 acres acquired on a lease that was negotiated post-war.

Helicopters at Chickerell

An interesting local incident occurred in May 1947 with a Hoverfly of a different Gosport-based squadron, but one that was later to be associated with Chickerell. Sub Lieutenant A.R.C. Beechener of No 705 Squadron, piloting helicopter serial number KL113 (the last one of the 45 Hoverflies supplied by Vought Sikorsky to the British Forces), had carried out a precautionary forced landing near the RAF radar station at Ringstead when he had indications of a loss of engine power whilst exercising in Weymouth Bay with the destroyer *HMS Rotherham*. Attempts to recover the aircraft by towing it across the soft ground where it had alighted failed, so it was flown at very low level (taxi-hovered) to the firmer road surface before being towed within the confines of the radar station for repair. The following day it flew back to Portland, where the 705 Sqn detachment was based at the former First World War seaplane hangar.

In these early post-war years, the airfield was used more by the FAA than the RAF. From September 1945 until some time prior to May 1947, the Rotary Wing Flight of No 771 Squadron, a Fleet Requirements Unit home-based at RNAS Gosport and equipped initially with the very basic R-4B Hoverfly helicopter, regularly flew from Chickerell on range duties and trials with HM warships. 771 Sqn continued to visit Chickerell on and off until disbandment in August 1955 – and would re-appear in the local area in 1961 when reforming at Portland with the Westland Whirlwind helicopter in the Search and Rescue role.

It was in September 1947 that the local waters saw another national 'first' for naval aviation, when 771 Squadron's Lt A. Bristow – later of Bristow Helicopters fame – carried out the first landing of a

Hoverfly KL113 air-taxies cautiously towards firmer ground. The masts behind the helicopter are the aerials of the Second World War RAF Ringstead radar station, which remained operational as part of the country's Air Defence Radar station chain until 1953.

helicopter on the stern of a small warship, the vessel being the modified River Class frigate *HMS Helmsdale* (K253), bringing back memories of the famous flight from *HMS Hibernia* in May 35 years earlier.

Accident off Portland

It is away from RAF Chickerell and its associated activities that we need to turn for a while, and on a sad note, for it was late on the morning of 6th May 1949 that the worst ever non-combat air accident occurred in the local area. That day Bristol Type 170 Type 21 Freighter G-AIFF was carrying out single engine climb tests some 16 miles off Portland in connection with an attempt to raise the maximum permitted (or certified) take-off weight of the aircraft. This was governed by the Civil Aviations Authority and based on demonstrated ability to climb safely away from the ground following a power plant failure during the take-off phase of flight.

Suddenly, a massive airframe failure occurred, caused by the overstressing of the tail fin. The crew of the submarine *HMS Truculent* (Lt Chalmers RN) saw the aircraft fall into the sea – with at least one large section detached from the main fuselage – only

Silver City Airways Bristol Freighter G-AIMA, sister aircraft to the ill-fated 'AIFF and 'AHJJ.

Silver City—the main commercial users of the Freighter operated the world's first air-carried car ferry service, between Lympe/Ferryfield airport in Kent and Le Touquet. The Royal New Zealand Air Force were the main military operators.

some four miles or so from where it was exercising, but of the seven crew members on board, under the command of Captain James Northway, none survived that last fatal dive. Despite an extensive search by *Truculent*, the two surface warships *HMS Zephyr* and *HMS Leeds Castle* and an RAF Coastal Command Lancaster only two bodies were recovered and, apart from the tail fin or rudder, and a control panel, virtually none of the main wreckage.

The crash occurred during the months leading up to the first flight of the prototype Bristol Brabazon airliner (G-AGPU). It was feared that the loss of the flight test crew members who gave their lives in G-AIFF (most especially Captain Northway, Bristol Aircraft's Assistant Chief Test Pilot, and Mr John Radclliffe, Head of the Brabazon Flight Research Department) might further delay this already late initial sortie. However, 4th September saw G-AGPU in the air for the first time but, unlike the Freighter, of which 214 were sold worldwide, the Brabazon was not a success and never entered commercial service. With the jet age dawning, an aircraft needing eight engines to give it the required performance was really never going to be financially or operationally viable. *If it don't look right, it don't fly right!*

A second Freighter (G-AHJJ) was lost in similar circumstances on 2nd March 1950, and all aircraft were then modified, retrospectively or on the production line, to strengthen the tail fin.

Squeezing through!
The *RAFV Mainmoor*, with ship's tender assisting, makes her way under the Town Bridge in January 1956, with the arch to her starboard jammed solid just above the down position.

Life on the Ranges

In July 1949 the safety rules for practice air to ground rocket attacks on the Chesil Bank Ranges were updated. The attacks were all to be carried out in a seaward direction, the aircraft normally to fly a left hand circuit pattern to keep it away from the Swannery. If a right hand circuit had to be flown, it had to be wide enough to go west of the Swannery and not over it. No weapons of any sort were to be dropped when flying parallel to the coast or towards it and finally, after the inter-service wrangling of the mid-1930s, the range boundaries were to be marked at sea by new Ministry of Transport approved buoys. Thus did the RAF Chesil Bank Bombing Ranges, with its support unit at Chickerell, move into the second half of the 20th century. Some Coastal Command Sunderland flying boat runs were however still flown parallel to the beach, so this rule seems to have been selective in its application.

It wasn't all progress, though, for travel across the Fleet between the mainland and the structures actually on Chesil Bank was still by rowing boat. A local fisherman, Harry 'Nimmo' Randall, was paid to maintain the boats and carry out minor repairs to the targets – which by the 1950s were rectangular rafts, painted 'Day-Glo Red' and each fitted with a red flashing light [80 flashes per minute] for night practice attacks.

For heavy maintenance the rafts were brought ashore on a slip at Ferrybridge. Occasionally they were also to be seen tied up in Weymouth Harbour.

Awaiting further tasking, the *RAFV Airmoor II* lies alongside the wall of the Outer Harbour, Melcombe Regis side – known as Custom House Quay.

Today the building with the ornate windows houses the Royal Dorset Yacht Club and the warehouse belonging to Allways Removals beyond the ship's bows is used by the Harbour Master, whilst the large four-storey warehouse astern of *Airmoor II* is now one of the resort's premier tourist attractions, 'The Deep Sea Adventure'.

Note the lack of any motor traffic!

The vessels mainly involved in moving the targets to and from the ranges were the *Moor* class mooring vessels – which were conversions from wartime motor minesweepers and the like – and of which the RAF possessed seven, including the five seen on different occasions in Weymouth Harbour between target movements: *Rafmoor*, *Airmoor*, *Mainmoor*, *Salmoor* and *Watchmoor*.

On 24th January 1956 *Mainmoor* was involved in a minor drama when moving from the Inner Harbour to the Outer, for the Weymouth side of the Town Bridge jammed in the almost-down position and the vessel had to squeeze through on the Melcombe Regis side of the waterway. This was probably her last time at Weymouth – but well into the 1980s she could still be seen as a mooring buoy tender at Newport Docks in South Wales, where she carried the name *Buoymoor* – but other RAFVs continued to call at Weymouth until at least the late 1960s.

'At the end of the day, we row and pray . . .'.
On a misty day in the 1950s, range personnel in the faithful rowing boat about to return to the mainland after plotting duty at one of the beach quadrant huts.

The crossing of the Fleet on a balmy summer's day was a pleasure; in winter, perhaps in pouring rain, wind-blown spray and with a vicious tide running it was a different matter, and personnel rarely reached either the beach or the mainland on return with dry uniforms, this despite the foul weather gear and sea boots issued to one and all!

In March 1958 a new quadrant building became operational on the mainland, doing away with the necessity of some of these crossings. On occasions, 'sunglaise' – the unit personnel's name for the sun reflecting off the sea, making it impossible to plot the explosion of the bombs – would render the range inoperable and allow the lads to relax in the sunshine or by canoeing on the Fleet.

On 1st January 1951 No 217 Signals Unit (Chesil Bank) [217 SU] was formed at RAF Bawtry, near Doncaster, and then moved down to Dorset to exercise radar range control of aircraft using the Lyme Bay/Chesil Bank facilities. On 20th February 1956 the unit was re-equipped with new Decca-built equipment. The 15th June 1959 saw 217 SU disestablished, only to immediately reappear as No 217 Mobile Signals Unit [217 MSU] and continuing to serve the ranges well after the Chickerell base had been closed down. For high altitude work the powerful air defence and military air traffic control radar unit at Sopley, West Hampshire, was often used to assist the mobile unit.

Amongst the units making regular use of the range facilities in the early 1950s was No 2 Air Navigation School, based at RAF Thorney Island. For example, one trainee navigator on a course running from October 1950 until September 1951 using Wellington T10 aircraft, flew 5 daytime bombing sorties off Chesil Bank, totalling some 13 hours, and another 7 hours on the range at night. Bombing was carried out from between 10,000 and 13,000 feet, using the Mk 11 bombsight and with 12 x 25lb practice bombs being dropped on each sortie.

The wartime aircrew trade of bomb aimer had by now been disestablished and all navigators were given training in basic bomb aiming skills. Today even the navigator, as such, is no more – for on 1st April 2003 all rear crew trades were merged to form the weapons system officer/operator specialisation.

On 2nd October 1952 Flying Officer R.G. Thomas MBE, already the unit's Second-in-Command, took over as Commanding Officer of 217 MSU from Flight Lieutenant Pangbourne, at which time its strength was in the order of 30 service personnel and two civilian staff. Operational Control of the ranges was exercised by Headquarters No 3 Group of Bomber Command, whilst responsibility for administration and domestic facilities was vested in RAF Merryfield, Somerset, a station in No 25 Group of Flying Training Command.

In July of the following year the ranges were closed on the 9th to allow MGM camera crews to shoot footage for the forthcoming film *The Dambusters*, whilst in the same month initial trails were carried out on the newly installed Gee-H (electronic) target facility.

'Unofficial' sign at the main gate in Radipole Lane in September 1950. The unit's official title was that of Royal Air Force Chesil Bank Bombing Range Unit.

Chickerell continues

Shortly after Queen Elizabeth II's Coronation on 2nd June 1953, the RAF hosted a party in the hangar for local school children, a highly successful event that still brings back fond memories today for those who attended it.

Throughout the 1950s light aircraft detachments to Chickerell were common place, with fixed or rotary wing aircraft from all three aviation arms of the British Armed Forces (Fleet Air Arm, Army Air Corps and Royal Air Force) being regular users of the Unit's airstrip – which had very little in the way of air traffic control or aerodrome safety facilities: radio (using the same frequency as the range control frequency), signal cartridges (should the radio fail) and just basic fire fighting kit.

The small hangar on the domestic side of the airfield, previously of an all canvas construction, had a metal roof fitted to it sometime between 1951 and 1953 to give better protection to the RN helicopters which had started to operate from Radipole Lane and required hangarage overnight and when not flying.

During this same period airmen from the unit, many of whom were National Service airmen, were used on occasions to carry out mock attacks on the Air Defence Radar station at RAF Ringstead – now in the front line of The Cold War – to test the unit's security procedures. RAF Ringstead closed down in 1953, at the same time as the new Rotor radar station on Portland became operational, but in order to provide an element of redundancy should Portland's new 'state of the art' kit give problems, the masts were not taken down until 1957.

Portland Rotor Radar Station

The Rotor radar site at RAF Portland was built between 1950 and 1951, one of eight stations of this type built during this period to replace or modernise wartime radars (such as the one at Ringstead).

The operations bunker was built deep in the dry moat/defensive ditch to the south of the Verne Citadel to provide some protection from the Soviet nuclear threat of the Cold War Years – an easier option, on the island, than digging into the ground, as was done with the UK's other new-build Rotor stations.

The main above-ground building, in addition to the seven radar towers and the generator buildings, was the main guardroom and control-of-access point, which was built to resemble a domestic bungalow as a form of camouflage. Below ground in the bunker were the main tracking room, workshops, telephone exchange (with direct links to the Fighter Command Sector Operations Centres), air conditioning plant, rest areas and the like. Normal access was via a lift down from the guardroom, supplemented by a staircase; an emergency exit came out on the east of Portland above the general area of the old Victorian East Wears gun battery.

RAF Portland, officially No 815 Signals Unit of No 11 Group of RAF Signals Command, was declared operational on 20th February 1953, with a peak number of 54 radar units in the Rotor chain being operational at any one time.

As radar technology advanced and intercept ranges increased dramatically, the number of stations in use fell away accordingly. Today there are less than six main RAF Ground Intercept Radar Units operational in the UK. This, the final Portland radar unit searching the skies rather then the seas for intruders, was operational for less than 6½ years.

Constructed to work alongside Portland Rotor Radar, an Anti-Aircraft Operations Room (AAOR) – a two storey, partially buried blockhouse in a former quarry on Ridgeway Hill (just to the east of the A354 Weymouth to Dorchester road) – was constructed at about the same time.

Overtaken by events, it was never used operationally, but saw considerable use by the Royal Navy as a map, chart and photograph store. The AAOR was sold off after the surface navy left Portland in 1995, whilst the Rotor site went into private ownership in October 2001. Of all the Rotor stations constructed, that on Portland is, by far, the one remaining in the best condition. As a survivor of the Cold War which dominated so much of the second half of the 20th century, it is now listed as a national monument.

Other radars on Portland had been located at RAF Westcliffe, on Priory Corner, (a Type 2 CHL radar, later replaced by a Type 15), at Portland Bill, and on former gun emplacements within the Verne Citadel itself. These latter radars were a Type 41 radar and a Type 54 radar, with a 200′ tower, with the PPI radar display being inside a nearby Nissen hut, and with a smaller hut accommodating the Lister 15kva generator and a separate brick building housing the more sensitive electronics and switchgear.

The Final Years

It was also in 1953 that the relatively minor changes to operating procedures on the ranges came under pressure from the Planning Committee of Dorset County Council. The Committee raised 'the strongest possible objections', on the grounds that the feeding grounds for the swans in the Fleet would be damaged, 'with possible disastrous effects upon the Abbotsbury Swannery, and that the amenities of the locality would be impaired'.

It is hard to understand how, just eight years after the cessation of a war which had at one time threatened the county with invasion and which airmen who trained at Chesil Bank had helped avert, the Councillors on the Committee could vote in so negative way. Dorchester Rural District Council responded in a much more understanding manner, asking only that it should be consulted prior to any major changes being initiated.

The main aircraft to use the ranges for bombing practice came from RAF Coastal and Bomber Commands, and included Sunderlands, Lancasters and Shackletons (Coastal Command) and Lincolns, Canberras and Valiants (Bomber Command).

Aircraft Movements at Chickerell and the Ranges

The following record of aircraft movements and other activities – taken in the main from the official Unit Diary (RAF Form 540) – gives some idea of life at Chickerell and on the range itself between January 1953 and the inevitable final closure in October 1959:

10 Jan 53   Two S-55 helicopters of 705 Sqn, FAA, made use of the airfield.

27 Mar 53   Members of the squadron were in attendance when HM King Hussein of Jordan visited the Westland Aircraft Factory at Yeovil, where the Sikorsky S-55 aircraft were being built under licence as Westland Whirlwinds.

24 Jul 53   Visiting helicopter from 705 Sqn departed for Gosport Naval Air Station (*HMS Siskin*).

17 Aug 53   One bombing sortie by a Coastal Command crew had to be aborted as the crew of the range launch were unable to light the target due to flat batteries. They were also unable to operate marine markers due to their inexperience.

During this month Type 1340 VHF radios became operational in the range control tower, with a back up set functional in the Radio Workshops at

Above Westland Dragonfly helicopter of 705 Sqn FAA, carrying the markings GJ706 and seen here on a snow dusted Chickerell airfield on a winter day in the early 1950s (probably 1954). GJ706 was not the aircraft's serial number: GJ indicated that Gosport was its home base, and the number between 700 to 711 that it was a 705 Sqn aircraft. Powered by an Alvis Leonides piston engine, the Dragonfly was a licence built version of the American Sikorsky S-51 aircraft.

Below Another view of the 705 Sqn Westland Dragonfly GJ706, this time airborne from Chickerell.

Chickerell for test purposes.

15 Sep 53   Airfield used by aircraft from Middle Wallop.

23 Sep 53   Airfield used for the day by 705 Sqn.

19-23 Oct 53   Airfield used by 706 Sqn Whirlwind HAS 22 aircraft.

8 Nov 53   Unit personnel participated in Remembrance Day Parade in Weymouth.

30 Nov 53   Helicopter from 705 Sqn attached for 14 days to take photographs of torpedo trials in Portland Harbour.

By November 1953 the range was being manned for up to 16 hours per day, with a minimum of 6 hours booking notice required for activation.

3 Dec 53   New radio frequency of 103.68 (Coastal Command VHF Common) added to current Range

Control Frequency of 122.22 Mc/s.

11 Dec 53 The 705 Sqn detachment ended and departed for *HMS Siskin*, Gosport.

During December 1953, two new quadrant huts were commissioned, a new generator was fitted at the range control tower and the number of radio sets available increased from two to six. New lighting was provided for the target marker arrows. The unit establishment was increased from 27 to 45 personnel.

26 Jan 54 One helicopter from 705 Sqn attached to work with the Home Fleet.

1-8 Feb 54 The Fleet was frozen over during this period and there was no access to the buildings out on the Bank itself.

4 Feb 54 705 Sqn aircraft returned to *HMS Siskin*.

5 Feb 54 Kit inspection!

22 & 25 Feb 54 Flt Lt Stradall of Dorchester Air Training Corps (ATC) visited Chickerell with a view to a new hut being sited there for the Weymouth Air Cadets – No 1606 Squadron.

Mar 54 No 1 'High Level' bombing target was replaced and the Gee-H target facility made available for general training use.

Early Mar 54 The ASW helicopters of 705 Sqn returned once more for training.

19 Mar 54 706 Sqn was renumbered as No 845 Squadron, on achieving operational status, and departed.

13 & 14 Mar 54 The Exercise Flight from the Light Aircraft School at RAF Middle Wallop – an Army unit based at an RAF station – carried out exercises on the airfield.

Apr 54 Fg Off RAD English (a Technical/ Armaments Officer) replaced Fg Off Thomas as Commanding Officer; the Senior NCO Range Controllers at this time were FS Spooner and Sgts Dagger and Harris.

Trials were carried out during the month on 'Bomb Plotting by Radar' – and the unit acquired its first television set!

27 Apr 54 Two aircraft from 657 Sqn, Army Air Corps (AAC), used the airfield (probably Austers).

24 & 25 May 54 Two Dragonfly helicopters of 705 Sqn FAA operated from the airfield. The pilots were Lt Cdr JC Jacob (Squadron Commander), Lt Symes and Lt Taylor.

22 & 23 Jun 54 Three aircraft of 657 Sqn flew from the airfield.

29 Jun 54 One Auster and one Beaver aircraft from Middle Wallop landed and departed.

Wing Commander L G Le B Croke CBE

Westland Whirlwind HAR 22 WV204 on trial at Chickerell in the 1950s – another licence built variant of an American helicopter, the Sikorsky S-55.

RAFVR(T) visited to view site of the proposed ATC hut. (Wg Cdr Croke had retired from the RAF as an Air Commodore and then served as the Officer Commanding Dorset and Wiltshire Wing of the ATC from 1947 to 1959.)

Jul 54 666 Sqn AAC (a Territorial Army [TA] unit) took part in *Exercise Scottish Sun* at Chickerell, with 100 personnel accommodated under canvas, operating 8 Austers and a single Chipmunk aircraft.

130 TA paratroopers carried out parachute jumps from a captive balloon on the airfield.

8 Jul 54 705 Sqn, FAA, – operating Dragonfly helicopters – flew from the airfield for just one day.

(During the period from May 1947 until Chickerell's closure in 1959, 705 Sqn flew Hoverfly, Dragonfly and Whirlwind helicopters; only some diary entries, such as this one, are specific as to the type of aircraft visiting.)

2-16 Jul 54 Ranges closed whilst No 6217 Bomb Disposal Unit swept and cleared them of unexploded ordnance.

4 & 5 Aug 54 Use was made of the airfield and Radipole Lane domestic site for *Exercise Round Up*.

9 & 10 Nov 54 Further *Exercise Round Up*, this time with participation by RAF Middle Wallop personnel.

Dec 54 The unit now had an establishment of one officer, 42 to 45 airmen and two civilians. Control was with HQ 3 Group, Bomber Command.

The Royal Navy at Portland, *HMS Osprey*, started to use parts of the airfield area as a sports ground (and continued to do so until closure).

1 Jan 55 RAF Weston Zoyland assumed temporary parenting responsibility for the unit from RAF Merryfield, which at this time was undergoing a change of roles on the disbandment of No 9

Tug-of-war at the summer 1954 'Open Day'. Note the large marquee in front of the houses in Radipole Lane. The RAF team came second, behind the Police champions.

Flying Training School.

Mar 55   Three aircraft movements carrying visiting officers from No 3 Group HQ.

Apr 55   Another single aircraft visit with officers from HQ 3 Group.

May 55   First record of a Percival Prentice (a two or three seat [depending on its role] basic training aircraft) landing at Chickerell.

Jun 55   During the month 1954 Flt, AAC, brought a 7 aircraft detachment to Chickerell, and the Air Observation Training School from Middle Wallop brought four of their Auster AOP aircraft in.

24 Jun 55   RAF Merryfield resumed parenting responsibility.

Jul 55   24 airmen from RAF Merrifield were accommodated on the unit whilst assisting in clearing up operations after disastrous local flooding along the valley running from the head of the River Wey down to the centre of the town of Weymouth and its suburbs.

(Author's note: 11 inches [280mm] of rain fell on the hills above Weymouth on the night of 18th/19th July, the greatest rainfall ever recorded in the British Isles in a 24 hour period).

Aug 5   One Auster and one Chipmunk from Middle Wallop used the airfield.

The range control frequency was changed from 143.37 Mc/s to 149.04 Mc/s, in the VHF aeronautical band.

Sep 55   One Chipmunk from RAF Colerne, and a Chipmunk and an Auster from Middle Wallop used the aerodrome.

1 Sep 55   Operational control of the unit was passed to HQ No 1 Group, Bomber Command.

18 Sep 55   The unit participated in the Battle of

De Havilland Chipmunk T10 WZ876 at Chickerell. Although bought initially as a basic training aircraft, Chipmunks were often used in the 1950s and early 1960s as light communications aircraft – hence, almost certainly, WZ876's presence on the airfield. This aircraft was one of the final batch of Chipmunks built for the RAF. It would seem to have been a windy day, for the aircraft can be seen to be piqueted.

Britain parade at St Edmund's Church, Weymouth.

Oct 55   One aircraft from Middle Wallop visited the airfield during a *Round Up* Exercise; there was also a single RN helicopter movement.

15 & 16 Nov 55   Austers from Middle Wallop participated in an 'end of course exercise'. The primary role of these aircraft was that of artillery spotting and such an exercise could involve working with Army units based locally at Bovington and East Lulworth. (The suffix 'AOP' used by the Austers meant 'Air Observation Post').

Dec 55   Flt Lt McGoughlin of No 37 ASRMCU, Lyme Regis, conducted a liaison visit to the unit.

12 & 13 Jan 56   AOP Austers from Middle Wallop at the airfield for *Exercise Round Up*.

12-31 Jan 56   Aircraft from the UK-based element of 848 Sqn, FAA, used the airfield for 'special training' duties.

10-29 Feb 56   848 Sqn continued its deployment to Chickerell airfield.

22 & 23 Feb 56   Further Middle Wallop visit for *Round Up*.

14 Mar 56   At the end of its deployment, 848 Sqn returned to its UK home base of Yeovilton, *HMS Heron*.

26-30 Mar 56   A single Whirlwind from the RAF's 22 Sqn, a search and rescue unit, was detached to the unit.

Apr 56   The 22 Sqn detachment continued.

15 May 56   The ongoing 22 Sqn detachment came

The entrance to the camp at Chickerell, with the airstrip visible below the base of the sign 'Royal Air Force Chesil Bank Range Unit'.

The large building just inside the gate was the Motor Transport Section and that beyond it the Communications Section. A hut to accommodate 1606 (Weymouth) Squadron of the Air Training Corps was later erected to the right of the MT building.

Today only the concrete 'bell mouth' at the gate remains, opening out on to busy Radipole Lane.

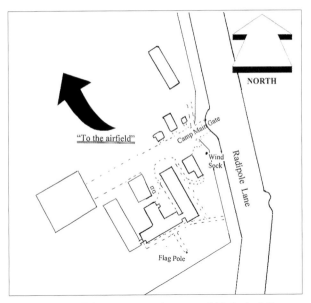

Sketch Map of the Accommodation and Technical Site at Chickerell(based on a 1951 aerial photograph and a 1957 OS map).

to an end.

23-31 May 56 A helicopter from RAF Defford, Worcestershire – a support airfield to the Royal Radar Establishment, Malvern – was deployed to Chickerell on a trial sponsored by the Ministry of Supply.

20 Jun 56 The Defford trial ceased and the aircraft returned to the Midlands.

27-29 Jun 56 Further use of the airfield by Middle Wallop based AOP aircraft.

9-23 Jul 56 Accompanied by a single Auster from Middle Wallop, the 14th Battalion The Parachute Regiment deployed to Chickerell for parachute training.

Sep 56 HQ Bomber Command closed the ranges for an unspecified period .

Dec 56 This month saw the unit establishment at its highest recorded level: one officer, 64 NCOs and airmen and 3 civilians.

Jan 57 The range control radios were upgraded to frequencies in the UHF band.

3-25 Jan 57 A three week detachment to the base by a single RN helicopter.

Apr 57 The unit was now being parented by RAF Sopley, in Hampshire, ('Southern Radar').

May 57 RN helicopters used the airfield on unspecified dates.

Sep 57 The gunnery facility on the range was withdrawn; all future activity would involve bombing practice only.

Mar 58 During the month the new Sergeants' Mess at Chickerell, and a new quadrant building, were taken over from the Air Ministry Works Department which had supervised their construction.

The unit strength at this time was one officer, 58 SNCOs and airmen and 6 civilian employees – 3 drivers, 2 kitchen hands and a range warden.

Apr 58 The new quadrant was declared operational and the new range observation and control tower came into use.

Author's note: the new control tower was located on the mainland near to the village of Fleet and replaced a three-storey ramshackle wooden building actually on Chesil Bank itself, which was demolished – the mainland location doing away with many of the laborious crossings of the Fleet lagoon previously necessary. Today, converted to a pleasant holiday home, the 1958 tower still stands adjacent to Sea Barn Farm camping ground [and similarly adjacent to one of the former target marker arrows].

9 Jun 58 An Auster from Middle Wallop landed carrying a visiting general.

Sep 58 Aircraft from 651 Sqn, AAC, used the airfield on and off throughout the month.

1-9 Sep 58 An RAF Balloon Unit operated on the airfield with members of the Parachute Regiment, who carried out a series of 'live jumps'.

During this summer an amusing incident – at

Church parades at the Chickerell Camp were a rarity. Here airmen parade prior to marching to Lanehouse Rocks Road for the dedication of St Edmund's Church in 1954.

least for those watching – occurred in Radipole Lane. Cadets of 1606 ATC Sqn were practising parachute landing procedures (specifically how to collapse the canopy in windy conditions) on the airfield outside their HQ, when two car drivers proceeding along Radipole Lane decided to watch the youngsters' antic – and collided head on at the junction with Hereford Road!

29 Sep 58   Radar plotting vehicle moved to a new site at Abbotsbury.

(**1 Oct 58**   The RAF station at Middle Wallop was transferred to the Army, to become the Army Air Corps Centre.)

16 Oct 58   Gp Capt Burton DSO MBE carried out the unit's annual inspection.

26 Nov 58   Plt Off Munn posted out to Headquarters Bomber Command; Flt Lt JM Stringer assumed temporary command of the unit.

Dec 58   Flt Lt T H Goacher DFM assumed command.

Feb 59   The RN from Portland were still using part of the airfield as a sports field, now having been joined by Royal Engineers from the nearby RE Bridging Camp (which is today known as The Wyke Regis Training Area).

21 & 30 Apr 59   651 Light Aircraft Sqn, AAC, used the airfield for joint exercises with the RN.

21 Apr 59   The AAC's 6th Independent Flight used the airfield for flying exercises.

29 Apr 59   Helicopters of 815 Sqn, FAA, used the airfield in connection with a flypast carried out in support of the visit by HM Queen and the young Prince of Wales that day to the aircraft carrier *HMS Eagle*, which was anchored out in Weymouth Bay.

(Author's note. As Princess Elizabeth, the Queen had launched *HMS Eagle* at Harland & Wolff's Belfast shipyard on 19 March 1946. During this visit to *Eagle*, the carrier's Sea Hawk and Sea Venom jets overflew the ship in an 'E II R' formation; Prince Charles reportedly took particular pleasure in sitting in one of the Fairey Gannet aircraft in the ship's cavernous hangar – the Gannet was the last fixed-wing anti-submarine warfare aircraft operated by the RN.)

27 Jul 59   RAF Portland, the former defence 'Centimetric Early Warning' Rotor radar station which had ceased to be operational in the late summer of 1958, was taken over by Chickerell's CO as an 'inactive site'.

Aug 59   The domestic site and married quarters at former RAF Portland were handed on to the Admiralty.

3 Sep 59   A signal (reference 'AR265') was received from HQ Bomber Command stating that the bombing range was to close and that the unit would be reduced to a Care & Maintenance status with effect from the 15th October. The range itself would be closed at midnight on the 11th.

18 Sep 59   Staff from RAF Sopley visited the unit to discus the closure.

24 Sep 59   Staff visit by officers from HQ Bomber Command and RAF Boscombe Down to define the future policy for the unit.

1 Oct 59   A Farewell Dinner was held – aptly because of its location overlooking the ranges – at the Moonfleet Hotel, on the outskirts of Chickerell village.

11 Oct 59   The Chesil Bank Bombing Range officially closed down. (The sea areas and airspace in parts of Lyme Bay, however, still remain as active danger areas to this day.)

15 Oct 59   With a unit establishment down to just one officer and 17 other ranks, the unit was now classified as being of Care & Maintenance status. The unit Landrover was to stay in the world of bombing ranges, being transferred to RAF Marham for use on the Holbeach Ranges by The Wash.

23 Oct 59   At 1700 hours, the Care & Maintenance Party having been officially stood down the previous day, the RAF ensign was lowered for the last time and "*the key was turned in the lock, the unit having been handed over to Flt Lt Downs of RAF Sopley*" (A direct quote from the F540).

8 May 63   All local Air Ministry assets associated

The main masts of the USAF Troposcatter Station at Ringstead, which were dismantled in 1973 after satellite technology rendered their use obsolete.

with the unit having been officially disposed of, RAF Sopley was relieved of its Inactive Site parenting responsibilities.

Range Aircraft

I have been lucky enough to see the log book of fighter controller Flight Lieutenant D.N.H. Parrott, who commanded the Mobile Radar Control Team covering Lyme Bay area for the period 2nd August 1957 until 21st May 1960 (by which time, of course, Chickerell itself had closed).

In the order in which they appear in his log book, the late Flt Lt Parrott records the following wide variety of aircraft types (26 in all) using the ranges: Hunter, Valiant, Gnat, Scimitar, Canberra, Shackleton, Sea Hawk, Gannet, Meteor, Swift, Javelin, Seamew, Vulcan, Hastings, Sea Vixen,

Firefly, Sea Venom, Provost, Whirlwind, Jet Provost, Victor, Harvard, Varsity, Dragonfly, Lightning, and Lincoln.

Aircraft duties, again in log book order, which the radar team controlled and provided safety surveillance for (both air and sea) included air-to-air and air-to-ground gun firing, sonobuoy exercises, air interceptions, fuel tank dropping trials, bombing, search and rescue apparatus (Lindholme Gear) drops, air-to-ground rocketry, flare dropping, guided missile releases, simulated depth charge drops, and paratroop drops. These statistics indicate just how busy and important the ranges were.

Americans at Ringstead

Not mentioned in the official Unit Diary (presumably for security reasons, for the Station Diary was only classified 'Restricted') was the fact that USAF personnel carrying out early works associated with the Troposcatter Station at Ringstead (just to the west of the former radar station) were accommodated at Chickerell in the late 1950s. With planning and research by these folk over, construction work on the huge aerial arrays commenced in 1961 and the station was operational from 1963 until 1972. Its aerials were dismantled in 1973.

Pre-dating most artificial satellites, the station's operational function was to 'bounce' UHF frequency signals off the various ionospheric layers – UHF suffered from range limitations but was not affected by atmospherics and sun spot activity as HF signals were. Signals went out from Ringstead to, normally, Rota in Spain, from whence they continued Stateside via The Azores. Incoming signals were routed by landline to Bullbarrow Hill, near Blandford Forum, (once an RAF unit and the Master Station for the Southern Gee Chain [an electronic navigation system]) and onwards to the USAF facility at RAF Croughton, in Oxfordshire.

Flying Boats in the Bay

In the post war years, until the RAF disbanded its final UK flying boat squadron, No 201 Squadron, at RAF Pembroke Dock in February 1957, Short Sunderland flying boats were occasionally to be seen anchored off the seafront in Weymouth Bay, a topic of conversation for holidaymakers and local residents alike. (201 Sqn is still a front line RAF squadron in the maritime role, and is now based at

Carrying the aircraft markings 'NS D', Sunderland Mk V VB889 of No 201 Squadron, in Weymouth Bay on a summer day during the early post war years.

The hotels at the Greenhill end of the Weymouth Promenade are clearly visible beyond, whilst the white-hulled Cosens pleasure craft alongside, proudly flying her 'red duster' would seem to be under short-term RAF charter; the other boats are hired rowing boats from the beach stalls.

Entering service too late to fly combat missions in the Second World War, this particular Sunderland was however a veteran of the Berlin Airlift. It was later transferred to No 235 Operational Training Unit at RAF Calshot.

RAF Kinloss in Scotland operating the 4-jet BAe Nimrod aircraft.) During one of the Sunderland visits – 28th July 1949 – the town's Mayor, Councillor A P Burt; Town Clerk, Mr P Smallman; and future Mayor, Edgar Wallis, enjoyed a flight in the local area in an aircraft captained by Flight Lieutenant David Hobdey, with the massive flying boat circling several times over the town, Weymouth Bay and Portland Harbour before alighting off the beach to discharge her passengers.

Chickerell's Future

As early as January 1959 Weymouth Town Council had started to discuss what it intended to do with the land at Chickerell on which it had a 'right to buy back' contract with the Air Ministry. The airfield site was in the Parish of Chickerell, outside the town boundary since the 1933 Boundary Review, but the town actually had owned the land prior to its pre-war takeover by the military.

Some members wanted the land to be used solely for housing, whilst other councillors favoured a division of the land, and both housing and industrial development, and it was this latter course of action that, by 17 to 13, took the vote.

It is interesting to note how this type of discussion on land formerly used for military purposes arose again in the 1990s, when the site of the former Whiteheads Torpedo Factory at Ferrybridge came up for disposal. Weymouth & Portland Borough Council wanted the site dedicated to light industrial use alone. No developer could be found willing to risk such an undertaking, and the site now boasts a fine selection of attractive houses, known as 'Harbour Point'.

Soon after Chickerell's closure, a public enquiry was held on the development plans that had been put forward. The Council's preferred option won the day and the land directly facing Radipole Lane was developed for housing – with two of the streets bearing aviation associated names: Cobham Drive (as already mentioned) and Stainforth Close. The rest of the land, a little further away from the older housing stock already in place, was turned over to light industry and is now called the Granby Industrial Estate.

This is still the *status quo* today, and other than the streets names, no remnant remains to be seen here of the RAF Chesil Bank Support Unit site – save for a small area of concrete in Radipole Lane at the former entrance to the camp.

Remembrance Day 1958, and shortly before moving from their accommodation at Chickerell for a new building in Barrack Road, near to the Nothe Fort, members of No 1606 (Weymouth) Squadron of the Air Training Corps parade along Weymouth Esplanade.

Saluting the Mayor's party is Squadron Commander Flight Lieutenant Jack Wolff DFC, who is followed by Warrant Officer Peter Price (left) and Flt Lt Stan Pitman. At the end of the Second World War Peter Price had served at Weymouth with No 40 ASRMCU.

Three Incidents

The story of the helicopters flying at the Portland Naval Air Station is beyond the scope of this book, but now is an opportune moment in our tale to mention three incidents related to Weymouth as well as to Portland.

On Tuesday 21st April 1959, three days before the official opening of the new helicopter base, the lifeboat maroons reverberated above the town and the *RNLB Frank Spiller Locke* prepared for sea – but her services were not wanted. A Whirlwind HAR Mk3 helicopter of 815 Sqn had suffered an engine failure near the Shambles Lightship and had ditched. The pilot Lt C. Gill and crewman Ldg Seaman C. Bartlett were plucked from the water by a ship's boat from the nearby *Blackwood* class frigate *HMS Keppel*, but the second crewman, AB Gerald Phillips, was sadly drowned.

1968 saw a further two local incidents involving Portland-based Whirlwinds. On Friday 28th May a 771 Sqn aircraft, XL878, suffered a major systems failure and crashed into the sea just off Weymouth's Stone Pier a few minutes after 8.00 am, the three man crew being in their inflatable life raft for less than 10 minutes before being winched to safety by a second helicopter.

On 9th October a second 771 Sqn Whirlwind was badly damaged, when XM665 – with Lt N.R. Anstis as pilot and PO W.E. Evans and Naval Airman T.E. Short as crew members – force-landed in the valley below White Horse Hill and rolled over on touchdown. None of the crew was injured; they left the scene in a second helicopter, with the downed aircraft being taken away by road later in the day.

In the spring of 1960 the target buoys were re-positioned, with the former No 3 buoy being sited between No 1 and No 2 buoys and the numbering changed to reflect the new orientation.

In February of the same year Charmouth Radar – No 217 MSU, of course – which was also known as the Lyme Bay Radar Unit, supported a Boscombe Down sponsored ejector seat and parachute trail, tracking the dummies as the fell from 15,000' to the surface and then using VHF radio to guide ASR launches from Lyme Regis to the impact points for recovery.

The Ranges Today

As far as the ranges themselves go, there are still active danger areas in Lyme Bay today (*see table on the right*), with EG D012 having horizontal limits

One of the very few reminders of the Bombing Range Unit: the final triangulation lookout built, which has been impressively converted to a holiday home adjacent to the Sea Camp holiday camp complex at Fleet. (On the ground nearby, one of the WWII target indicator arrows can still be seen.)

very similar to the former 'Chesil Bank Bombing & Gunnery Ranges':

Danger Area Designator	Vertical Limits	Activities normally carried out
EG D012	Surface level up to 18,000', with occasional activity up to 25,000'.	Air Firing and Bombing
EG D013	Surface level up to 60,000'.	Air Firing, Bombing, Pilotless Target Aircraft and Ship Exercises
EG D014	Surface level up to 5,000', with occasional activity up to 15,000'.	Bombing, Missile Firing and Ship Exercises.
EG D017	Surface level up to 22,000', with occasional activity up to 55,000'.	Pilotless Target Aircraft, Firing and Ship Exercises.

Occasionally seen in the skies over Weymouth are (*Top*) the sophisticated S-61N of HM Coastguard, airborne from Portland – the busiest coastguard helicopter base in the British Isles: (*Centre*) the McDonnell Douglas MD902 Explorer operated by the Dorset Police; and (*bottom*) the Bolkow 105 DBS helicopter of the Dorset and Somerset Air Ambulance, seen here in a field near Dorchester to receive casualties from a road accident.

The Weymouth skies

Although the RN helicopter base at Portland closed in 1999, the skies above Weymouth are not completely denuded of rotary-wing aircraft movements. In addition to the Merlins, Sea Kings and Lynxes transiting between RNAS Yeovilton (*HMS Heron*) and exercise areas south of Portland Bill, three different helicopters can be seen operating in emergency and life-saving roles of one form or other.

Firstly one occasionally hears the reassuring clatter of the Sikorsky S-61N helicopter based on the former naval air station at Portland and operating in the Search and Rescue role for HM Coastguard. Then there are the aircraft operated by the Dorset Police and the Dorset and Somerset Air Ambulance. The police aircraft are based at Police Headquarters at Winfrith, whilst the Air Ambulance base is at Henstridge, a former RN wartime airfield (*HMS Dipper*) on the Dorset/Somerset border.

With Weymouth lying to the south and to the east of two of the major airways crossing southern England, the person looking skywards from the Weymouth area to a cloud free sky will usually see one or more condensation trails from jet airliners making their way to and from the North Atlantic Oceanic Control Area, en route the USA and Canada, or to and from continental Europe – the contrails at their most attractive as they glisten pink at dawn or dusk.

Whence and where to? We cannot tell from ground level – a Boeing 747 inbound to Paris from Vancouver, an Airbus just levelling out at its cruising level on departure from Amsterdam for New York or a humble Boeing 737 with its load of happy holidaymakers on their way from Glasgow to Malaga? It's just fun to watch and dream!

At a lower level, the fixed wing aircraft most commonly seen overhead are the pretty little Dassault Falcon 20 twin-jets of FR Aviation, as the make their way back to their base at Bournemouth International Airport when weather conditions allow for a 'visual/non-procedural recovery'. The task of these aircraft and their crews is to provide electronic warfare training for – mainly, but not exclusively – ships of the Royal Navy. FR Aviation is part of the Cobham plc group, so even after all these years the memory of Sir Alan still lives on locally in a practical way.

FIVE

No 40 Air Sea Rescue and Marine Craft Unit, Weymouth

No 40 Air Sea Rescue and Marine Craft Unit (ASRMCU) was formed at Weymouth on 6th April 1944 under the command of Flt Lt W G Howes. The unit's first two marine craft, High Speed Launches (HSLs) 2696 and 2697, arrived from Dover on 20th April with HSL2694 arriving in the port one day later.

The standard colour scheme for the vessels was one of a black hull (above the anti-fouling), and grey decks and superstructure, with an RAF roundel on either side of the bows immediately ahead of the pennant number, which was also painted on the stern. A larger roundel was usually painted on the foredeck to assist in identification from the air.

The unit was declared operational on 27th April, with the crews initially sleeping aboard their vessels, but messing with the Royal Navy at *HMS Grasshopper* – Weymouth Naval Base, with its headquarters in the 'closed for the duration' Pavilion Theatre (re-opened post war as the Ritz, destroyed by fire in 1954, rebuilt and renamed the Pavilion).

The messing arrangements proved impracticable, so rations were drawn instead and then cooked on the boats – it was probably administratively inconvenient as much as anything else to do otherwise, for on 28th April *HMS Grasshopper* had been handed over to the US Navy as local preparations for D-Day intensified.

Later on the off duty personnel were messed and accommodated at the domestic site at Chickerell airfield. For at least part of the time that it was operational, the unit's headquarters and operations room was in the old Customs House building, now the home of 'Portland Coastguard'. Refuelling was normally carried out within the confines of Portland Harbour rather than alongside at Weymouth.

The unit's first 'crash calls' were on 7th (2 calls) and 24th May, but all three searches were abortive – although they gave the crews the opportunity of working together under operational conditions. Weymouth, even in the early summer of 1944, was still very much in the front line, and on 27th May Cpl Boreham was injured in an air raid on the town and hospitalised.

Weymouth-based 'Whaleback' high speed launch showing her paces as she planes across a relatively calm sea at a speed in the order of 30 knots. Note the two defensive ·303" gun turrets, similar to those in bomber aircraft, but not hydraulically powered.

HSL 168 survived the war, was later converted to a remotely controlled target vessel and was the last but one 'Whaleback' to be struck off charge – on 31st January 1950.

On D-Day itself Weymouth launches were positioned offshore ready to assist any casualties from the massive air armada flying overhead including, of course, gliders and tugs from the Dorset airfield of RAF Tarrant Rushton – from whence the first troops to land on D-Day took off (soldiers of the Ox & Bucks Light Infantry, under the command of Major John Howard, who took the bridges over the River Orne and the Caen Canal [the canal bridge later to be known as Pegasus Bridge] at Bénouville).

Unfortunately, the pre-positioning of the boats seems not to have been known to all whom it should have been – for at just after 8.00 am HSLs 2691 and 2697 were attacked by six Beaufighter aircraft to the south of St Aldhelm's Head. Fortunately, this 'Blue on Blue' incident did little damage to the launches!

The following day four injured US airmen were brought ashore from *HMS Skate*; then, on the 11th, 40 ASRMCU carried out its first actual rescue, one airmen being rescued by HSL2691 – with sister ship 2697 finding only two empty life rafts at the same datum.

Non-Weymouth based RAF ASR vessel at speed off the Nothe headland after calling at 40 ASRMCU whilst in transit to a West Country base.

The rest of June was equally busy:

10th: One injured man was brought ashore from a vessel in Weymouth Bay by HSL2694.

11th: HSL2707 took a Mustang pilot off a destroyer south of Portland Bill and landed him at Portland.

11th: The crew of HSL2696 spotted an aircraft in obvious difficulties before it ditched, but only one survivor was found despite the prompt response.

12th: HSL2696 proceeded to a reported crash 5 miles north east of Portland Bill, picked up the pilot

After VE Day, by which time the unit was under the command of Fg Off, later Flt Lt, Terry, it became the practice for one of the Weymouth vessels to be detached to the Channel Islands on a weekly rotation. Here we see Weymouth-based LRRC 040, formerly MTB 744, lying quietly alongside the harbour wall at St Peter Port, Guernsey.

and landed him at Portland.

15th: Whilst holding in her patrol area, the crew of HSL2697 saw an explosion some 11 miles south of Portland Bill. They closed the vessel, an RN destroyer, and took 3 officers and 37 ratings, many of them injured, off her stern before proceeding to Portland with them.

15th: HSLs 2691 and 2707 landed 45 survivors at Portland. The records remaining today are imprecise, but this was probably the same warship and was probably a destroyer that had suffered major damage when hitting a mine off the Channel Islands on this date.

22nd: HSL2697, with 2696 in support, towed a Walrus flying boat to Portland which had carried out a landing in Weymouth Bay and had then become fouled on the anchor cable of a landing craft. Aboard the aircraft were its three crew and a single survivor who had earlier been rescued by the Walrus.

Both of the noteworthy events which occurred in July 1944 involved HSL2694. On the 20th she put to sea to take nine survivors off *HMCS Q'Appelle* – the survivors being crew members of *US Tug 75*, which had become lost in fog off the Channel Islands and come under gunfire from the German coastal defence batteries on Alderney. The rescued sailors were landed at Portland.

Four days later, on 24th July 1944, the Unit Diary records that the crew of the same launch recovered the body of a Fg Off Ollett, which they came across whilst searching for another aircraft – the crew of which was rescued by a Walrus. The only Fg Off Ollett recorded as losing his life at about this time in the war was Fg Off James Frederick Ollett of No 179 Squadron, a unit flying both Warwick V and Lancaster ASR3 aircraft in the air sea rescue role, who died on Saturday 24th June 1944. I suspect that this must be one and the same person, for there is no indication as to how long the body recovered in July had been in the water. Another tragic casualty of war, Fg Off Ollett, a married man, now lies at rest in his native Derbyshire.

On 3rd October Pinnace 78 rescued the two crew members of a Barracuda aircraft, which had ditched just off Portland Harbour's Breakwater Fort. They were both uninjured and, after being landed at Weymouth, were taken to RAF Warmwell by ambulance.

The following day, Flt Sgt Currie and Cpl Wealthdale, together with US Seaman N Caly (of USS LST529) rescued a young widow from

Weymouth Harbour who had apparently attempted suicide.

By November 1944, the original launches at the unit had all gone, having been replaced by three 63' 'Whaleback' HSLs – 184 (Captain: Fg Off Jones), 185 (Flt Lt Farr), and 168 (Fg Off Crosby). The unit strength was 4 officers and 54 NCOs and airmen.

After a quiet start to 1945 (with just one call out, responded to by HSL185, on 23rd March for the crew of a Beaufighter aircraft which crashed on the Chesil Bank Bombing ranges), one of the most unusual call outs received by the unit came on 6th July – Weymouth being involved as the No 36 ASRMCU, based at Poole, had by now been stood down.

An American Navy PBY Catalina flying boat was reported down in the sea some seven miles south east of Bournemouth with engine trouble, and HSL2509 was scrambled to the scene. Both of the PBY's engines had run out of oil. A Noorduyn Norseman aircraft, almost certainly an American one, as those allocated to the RAF under Lend-Lease seem all to have been retained in Canada, dropped drums of oil to the stranded flying boat and 2509 herself passed across two 15 gallon drums of oil. The sumps topped up, the Pratt & Whitney Twin Wasp radial piston engines were restarted and the PBY taxied into Poole Harbour escorted by the RAF launch.

This was the last life-saving/productive service by 40 ASRMCU, although the final call out came on 6th August when an aircraft crashed near No 1 Target off Chesil Beach – but the pilot's body was recovered by a local fishing boat before the HSL

In the centre in this 1945 photograph is the *PS Embassy*, recently returned to her home port after minesweeping service as *HMS Ambassador*. One the right, tied up alongside Customs House Quay, are Air Sea Rescue vessels HSLs 2615 and 2633 and possibly, just discernable in the sea of masts and superstructures, also HSL 2613. All three of these launches left Weymouth on 5th October 1945: 2615 and 2633 both went to No 54 ASRU on the Isle of Man, whilst 2613 went to Calshot.

arrived on scene.

The final vessels allocated to the unit were Long Range Rescue Craft (LRRC) 014 and 015 which were conversions of Fairmile motor torpedo boats (MTBs), and it was these two modern rescue craft, with occasional relief vessels, which continued to serve at Weymouth until the unit's disbandment on 15th June 1946. Coincidentally, that same day the ferry service from Weymouth to The Channel Islands resumed after the war cessation – the *St Helier* (Captain R R Pitman), a proud veteran of the Dunkirk evacuation of June 1940, sailing from the port that same Saturday evening.

The Sea Shall Not Have Them. This was the motto of the RAF's Air Sea Rescue Branch – and No 40 ASRMCU helped in its own modest way to achieve that commendable aim, by directly saving 11 downed aircrew, by bringing ashore 99 survivors from other vessels which had rescued them, and by saving the life of an unhappy widow who tried to drown herself in Weymouth Harbour. It was a record to be quietly proud of.

SIX

Aircraft Accidents on the Chesil Bank Bombing Ranges

The information listed here is taken from RAF Flying Accident Cards (where available), reports from the *Dorset Daily Echo*, the personal records of Wg Cdr D.R. Collier Webb RAF (Retd) and from records held at the RAF Museum, Weymouth Public Library's 'Local Collection', the Public Records Office, Kew, and at the Dorset County Public Records Office, Dorchester.

Tuesday 28th May 1907

War Department (Army) Balloon '*Thrasher*'.
Crew members: Lt W.T.M^c. Caulfield and Lt T E Martin-Leake, Royal Engineers.
Unit: Army Balloon School, Aldershot (Operating from Farnborough).
The craft had lifted off at 4.22 pm to demonstrate ballooning to King Edward VII and his guest Prince Fushimi, and was seen to drift generally in a westerly direction, the crew later speaking to people on the ground as it passed Dorchester.
It was observed by the Abbotsbury Coastguard as it passed overhead its lookout station, shortly after which, at about 8.30 pm, the Coastguard Officers saw the *Thrasher* drop into the waters of Lyme Bay and rise back into the air again. It is assumed that both crew members were thrown into the sea during the initial impact – or leapt out in a vain attempt to swim ashore – for sadly neither survived,

Lt Caulfield's body being picked up off Wyke Regis on 23rd June and Lt Martin-Leake's being washed ashore on the Chesil Bank six days later. The wreckage of the balloon had been recovered on the day after the accident by the fishing boat *Skylark* and landed at Brixham.

Lts Caulfield and Martin-Leake are commemorated on a memorial window in the Cathedral Church of the Bishop of the Forces, St Michael and St George at Aldershot in Hampshire.

The stained glass Memorial Window in what was, at the time of the window's dedication, The Aldershot Garrison Church of St George. The text reads 'In memory of Lieutenants T.E. Martin-Leake and W.T.M^c. Caulfield Royal Engineers. Drowned at sea in H.M.Balloon 'Thrasher'. May 28 1907. Erected by past and present officers of the Balloon School'. The window was unveiled by Brigadier General P.T. Buston, Chief Engineer, and dedicated by the Bishop of Winchester.

Saturday 11th December 1937

Fairey Battle Mk 1; serial number K7594.
Pilot: Sgt Arthur William Butler.
Gunner: Aircraftman 2nd Class William Ernest Vincent.
Unit: No 226 Squadron, RAF Harwell (Detached to No 8 Armament Training Camp, RAF Woodsford [later renamed RAF Warmwell to avoid confusion

with the Avro factory airfield at Woodford, near Manchester]).

When the aircraft arrived at the range the 'Standby' signal was still being displayed, and whilst holding off for the 'Clear to Fire' signal to be displayed (*see note below on* Range Visual Signals), the pilot flew low and fast over the target area at between 200' and 300'. At some point the starboard undercarriage leg was seen to be extended and this may have contributed to the loss of airspeed which caused the aircraft to spin in from low level.

The mission described was one of gunnery practice against the ground target using the light bomber's rear gun (a Vickers ·303" 'K' gun).

The aircraft crashed at Herbury Point, both crew members being killed on impact.

This was the RAF's 89th fatal accident of 1937, with 143 lives being lost by that date.

Range Visual Signals

When the range was clear two balls were raised on a mast. If the range controller wished the pilot to stop firing for any reason, one ball was lowered and if he wished to pilot to depart from the range the other ball was lowered and the target closed (by folding in the target marker strip). Red Very lights could be used as well. If a pilot flew too low a black flag was flown and if he flew too low again [the base level was normally 200 ft] he would be sent off the range.

Wednesday 25th May 1938

Hawker Fury Mk 1; serial number K8223.
Pilot: Pilot Officer Keith Hunter.
Unit: Probably No 9 Flying Training School, RAF Hullavington, Wiltshire (Detached to No 8 Armament Training Camp, RAF Warmwell).
The aircraft was one of three carrying out an early morning air-to-air gunnery exercise over the ranges when an in-flight fire occurred. Although suffering from burns, Plt Off Hunter was able to bail out of the biplane trainer by parachute and landed in the sea about half a mile off Chesil Bank.

A brave attempt to rescue the airman by Royal Engineers troops from the Bridging Camp had to be abandoned because of the swell and under current, but within 10 minutes or so, despite the heavy seas, the range safety launch (from No 37 ASRMCU, Lyme Regis) was on the scene and retrieved the pilot from the water. He was then transferred to a naval destroyer for medical aid and taken on to Portland for admission to the RN Hospital.

Westland Wallace Mk II K6084 at an armament practice camp at RAF Warmwell in 1938. This aircraft bore the next-in-sequence serial number to that which crashed whilst under the command of Plt Off Robinson.

Saturday 10th December 1938

Hawker Fury Mk 1; serial number K8271.
Pilot: Corporal John Robert Daniel.
Unit: No 9 Flying Training School, RAF Hullavington, Wiltshire (Detached to No 8 Armament Training Camp, RAF Warmwell).
The aircraft crashed into the waters of the Fleet opposite Fleet House (now the Moonfleet Hotel) during an air-to-ground gunnery exercise after the tail struck the top layer of pebbles on the Chesil Bank as it climbed away after its second firing pass at the target.

The pilot was killed on impact, his body being recovered from the aircraft later in the day and taken to Weymouth & District Hospital.

Friday 10th March 1939

Westland Wallace Mk II; serial number K6063.
Pilot: Pilot Officer Robinson.
Crewman: Leading Aircraftman Baker.
Unit: No 6 Armament Training School, RAF Warmwell.
The aircraft was acting as a drogue-towing target when it was seen to be in difficulties and attempting to make a forced landing in a field between Chickerell and Langton Herring. It hit a stand of trees as it came to rest and caught fire. Both occupants, who had escaped serious injury, attempted in vain to extinguish the fire that had broken out on impact, but the aircraft burnt out. An RAF ambulance from RAF Warmwell later arrived on the scene and took the aircrew back to camp.

Overstrand K4563 at RAF Warmwell, almost certainly before or after a training sortie on the Chesil Beach Ranges. The large number of groundcrew in attendance indicates a technical problem waiting to be solved! K4563 was one of the early Overstrands delivered to the RAF, whereas the ill fated K8173 was of the final 1937 batch.

Monday 13th March 1939

Hawker Audax; serial number K4396.
Pilot: Acting Pilot Officer Adam de Pencier.
Unit: No 6 Flying Training School, RAF Little Rissington, attached to No 6 Armament Training School, RAF Warmwell.

Plt Off de Pencier, the son of the Archbishop of New Westminster, British Columbia, was carrying out air-to-ground gunnery on the range when, at about 3.30 pm, he failed to pull out of a dive and hit the top of the beach, somersaulted and crashed into the sea some 20 yards beyond the target.

The aircraft caught fire after the impact and de Pencier's body was only recovered after an extensive operation involving the marine craft serving the range and a party of some 50 personnel from RAF Warmwell.

The detachment from Little Rissington had only arrived at Warmwell that same morning and de Pencier was one of the first to fly across to the range, although he had visited the range by car before his sortie. Both the RAF Inquiry and the civil Coroner's Court came to the conclusion that the accident was caused by an error of judgement.

Plt Off de Pencier lies at rest in the Commonwealth War Graves Commission plot at Holy Trinity Church, Warmwell – the only non-Second World War burial in the plot.

Wednesday 12th July 1939

Single seat aircraft; type and serial number unknown.
Pilot: 2nd Lieutenant Nuri Muhsin, Royal Iraqi Air Force, attached to an RAF Flying Training School.

It would appear that Lt Muhsin, who was flying solo, was engaged in an air-to-air gunnery sortie and possibly 'overtook' the sleeve target being towed by the target aircraft, became entangled in the tow cable and suffered a major structural failure.

His aircraft crashed at 8.00 am two miles offshore, near to the site of the wreckage of the ill fated aircraft-carrying submarine M2. Two RAF launches promptly arrived at the crash scene, marked by a spreading film of oil and fuel, and were later joined by three trawlers from the Portland Naval Base, but were unable to effect a rescue.

Over the next two days the trawlers, assisted by the RMAS tug Pilot, attempted to 'grapple' the aircraft from the seabed, but to no avail – the severe West Bay currents hampering all efforts.

22nd April 1940

Boulton Paul P75 Overstrand Mk 1; serial number K8173.
Pilot: Pilot Officer David Raymond Williams.
Crew Members (2): Not recorded by name.
Unit: No 10 Bombing & Gunnery School, RAF Warmwell.

The Overstrand was the first RAF aircraft to be fitted with a power operated defensive gun turret, but by 1940 the few Overstrand bombers remaining in RAF service had been relegated to training duties – such as the bombing practice which Plt Off Williams was conducting. As an operational bomber the aircraft had carried a crew of five; however only three airmen were on board K8173 when it crashed.

At 11.30 am on the day in question, the aircraft was observed in a steep turn, with flames coming from the port engine. One crew member – not the pilot – parachuted from the aircraft as it fell vertically into the sea, but he was (contrary to orders) not wearing a life jacket and drowned before the range safety boat reached him.

The mortal remains of Plt Off Williams were never recovered. He is commemorated on the Air Forces Memorial at Runnymede (on the hill above the site of the signing of the Magna Carta, by the River Thames), where over 20,000 of those who gave their lives in the skies over the United Kingdom and North & West Europe, and who have no known resting place, are remembered.

22nd April 1940
Fairey Seal Mk 1; serial number K3525.
Pilot: Sergeant C Barrett.
Crewman: Not recorded.
Unit: No 10 Bombing & Gunnery School, RAF Warmwell.
Target towing exercise completed, Sgt Barrett flew to the target dropping-off field, between Chickerell and Langton Herring, to release his drogue. Drop completed, he executed a climbing turn from low level, stalled the aircraft in the turn and crashed into the field below, where the aircraft caught fire. Sgt Barrett was killed, but his crewman survived the crash and was admitted to hospital.

23rd April 1940
Westland Lysander Mk II; serial number L4799.
Pilot: Pilot Officer 'Paddy' Barthropp.
Observer/Gunner: AC1 W C Holloway.
Unit: No 613 (City of Manchester) Squadron.
The Lysander was returning to Chickerell after flying an anti-invasion patrol, short of fuel, and found Chickerell covered by a blanket of very low hill fog.

When the AC Holloway refused to bail out, Plt Off Barthropp let down blindly through the murk at 50 to 55 mph until finally hitting terra firma half a mile north of the Chickerell landing ground. Both crew members walked away uninjured from the wreckage, which was subsequently classified as a write off.

A pristine L4799 in happier days, with groundcrewman or, possibly observer/gunner before all aircrew were given NCO status, alongside and with a further Lysander in the background. The Lysander wears 613 Sqn's early wartime code 'ZR', but no individual aircraft code letter. Nice as it would be to think that this photograph might have been taken at Chickerell, despite the aircraft standing on grass and not concrete, there is no other evidence to suggest this.

7th May 1940
Fairey Seal; serial number K3480.
Pilot: Sergeant A Y McCombe.
Crew members (2): Not recorded.
Unit: No 10 Bombing & Gunnery School, RAF Warmwell.
(This aircraft accident didn't actually happen in the area of the ranges, but is included in this listing as it was directly associated with the ranges.)

The aircraft had just taken off from RAF Warmwell en-route the ranges to act as target-towing aircraft for an air-to-air gunnery exercise when it suffered a failure of its Panther engine. Too low to bail out and with no suitable area ahead in which to carry out a successful forced landing, Sgt McCombe was committed to putting down in an area of marshland – causing damage to both aircraft and occupants!

All three crew members were hospitalised, whilst K3450 was classified as being 'repairable at a maintenance unit or contractor's works'.

Next aircraft off the production line after RH752: here Brigand RH753 is undergoing maintenance. The aerodynamic structure seen below the wing is not an airbrake – such as probably led to the loss of RH752 – but a trailing edge flap, used to augment lift at slow speeds.

fragments breaking through the side of the fuselage and rupturing hydraulic pipe lines. This resulted in a total loss of hydraulic fluid and the aircraft having to land back at Boscombe Down with, both, flaps and undercarriage retracted.

Neither crew member was injured in the 'belly landing', but the aircraft was seriously damaged.

Sunday 5th December 1943

Boeing B-17 Flying Fortress; serial number 42-3297 (*The Bad Penny*).
Pilot: 2nd Lieutenant N.M. Palmer
Unit: 571st Bombardment Squadron, RAF Framlingham, Suffolk

This United States Army Air Force heavy bomber ran out of fuel and ditched off the beach near the Abbotsbury Coastguard Station, the crew (who were on their first operational mission) being rescued by local boatmen. The aircraft was one of 548 dispatched by the 388th Bomber Group to bomb the aircraft assembly works at Bordeaux.

The two fishermen who saw the crash put to sea in their rowing boat. Two men were in the water supporting a third, another was drifting away in a life raft and the other six were standing on the sinking fuselage. All were brought safely ashore, but sadly, and despite the efforts of the local doctor, the left waist gunner – S/Sgt Everett Hanna – died on the beach, probably from shock and exhaustion.

The local Hutchinson family, who paid a major role in the rescue and subsequent treatment of the crew, were recompensed for their costs in food and sheets torn up to use as bandages to the tune of 5 shillings and 9 pence (c29p) by the UK authorities, and to food and bedding by the grateful USAAF.

23rd March 1945

No 40 ASRMCU, Weymouth, has an entry in its Operations Record Book stating that an abortive search was carried out by HSL185 for the crew of a Beaufighter aircraft that had crashed on the ranges, but no other details are given.

6th August 1945

No 40 ASRMCU's ORB has an entry for this day recording the fact that an aircraft crashed near to the Chesil Bank No 1 target, and that the pilot was killed and his body recovered by a fishing boat before the Weymouth rescue craft arrived on the scene.

19th July 1947

Bristol Brigand Mk I; serial number RH752.
Pilot: Flight Lieutenant Thomas William George Morren.
Air Gunner: Flight Lieutenant Ian John Hartley.
Unit: B Squadron, Armament Test Squadron, Aircraft & Armaments Experimental Establishment, RAF Boscombe Down.

The Brigand was conceived as the replacement for the successful torpedo-bomber version of the Beaufighter, and served with the RAF in this, and a variety of other roles, until 1958.

RH752 was participating in an air firing experiment over Lyme Bay and crashed into the sea, breaking up on impact, during the pull-up manoeuvre at the end of a firing dive. It was surmised that only one dive brake retracted on pull up and that, as a result of this, the aircraft flicked over and that the pilot was unable to regain control before it hit the sea in a spiral dive. The crew were posted as missing, presumed killed, and are both commemorated on the Air Forces Memorial at Runnymede.

Overnight on 4th/5th June 1951

Short Sunderland GR Mk V; serial number EJ153; side letters DQ.
Captain: Sqn Ldr J.T. Ormston.
Unit: No 235 Operational Conversion Unit, RAF Calshot.

As part of the crew's 'conversion to type', Sunderland flying boats from 235 OCU carried out practice bombing exercises on the ranges, the pilots dropping the bombs by day from as low as 50 feet

Preparations underway to bring Sunderland EJ153 ashore at RAF Calshot after her lucky escape from the clutches of the Dorset countryside in 1951.

and the navigators carrying out night attacks from 300 feet above the sea, the latter taking aim from the perspex nose position below the front gun turret.

On this occasion the trainee crew, flying solo (ie: without an OCU Staff 'screen' pilot) was positioning, at night, for its second drop when the pilots flew in too far over the adjacent land and struck high ground a glancing blow near Abbotsbury: two feet lower and there would have been a catastrophic crash; two feet higher and nobody onboard would have realised how close they had come to a premature death!

The crew had plenty of fuel so remained airborne until after daybreak, when observers on the ground at Calshot could see the damage to the lower hull that the crew had already reported. Offered the option of bailing out, the crew declined and the aircraft was eased back onto a shallow part of Southampton Water, but instead of being taxied sedately to its mooring, the flying boat was taxied up to the beach adjacent to the Flight Mechanics crew room before it could sink.

The crew retained dry feet throughout, the Sunderland was salvaged when the tide fell and beaching trolleys could be utilised, and was returned to service before the year was out, and (by then bearing the side marking the single letter 'D') was finally struck off charge in November 1956. What could have so easily been the worst ever crash on the bombing range was, luckily, just a scare for the crew!

Water gushes from the damaged hull of EJ153 as she sits on her beaching legs at Calshot. The number and size of the holes indicates the force with which the Sunderland clipped the Abbotsbury hillside.

Sqn Ldr John Ormston went on from the OCU course to command No 205 Squadron in Singapore – the RAF's last flying boat squadron. 235 OCU closed down on 17th October 1953, the residual flying boat training commitment being taken over by RAF Pembroke Dock, in South Wales.

15th July 1968

Hawker Hunter Mk F7; serial number WV253.
Pilot: Lieutenant C A Wheal, RN.
Unit: Empire Test Pilots School, Boscombe Down.
WV253 was the first Mk F7 Hunter, being a conversion from a Mk4. On the day of the accident, Lt Wheal – a Fixed Wing Course student at the ETPS – was carrying out a spinning and recovery exercise as part of his test pilot training, when he was unable

Photographed from the chase aircraft, here we see WJ632 in happier times in September 1966, on the first flight of the Flight Refuelling Ltd's Rushton Winch – one winch being located below each wing. British Aerospace pilot Johnny Squier and FR's Dennis Lewis were the crew members.

to recover from an intentional 'erect' spin which went horribly wrong and was forced to eject.

The aircraft, a single seat day fighter, crashed off Humble Point, between Seaton and Lyme Regis; Lt Wheal was rescued from the waters of Lyme Bay by a fishing vessel.

(Although the bombing ranges in their original form had closed back in September 1959, Danger Areas were still promulgated as 'active' in Lyme Bay – and continue as such today.)

1st May 1970

English Electric Canberra TT18; serial number WJ632.
Pilot: Major J R Weaver USAF.
Navigator: Flight Lieutenant J Nicol.
Observer: Flight Lieutenant G W E Foster AFM.
Unit: B Squadron, Aircraft & Armament Experimental Unit, RAF Boscombe Down.
The Canberra was the world's first jet-powered bomber aircraft, its maiden flight being on 13th May 1949. This particular aircraft was the first Mk B2 (bomber) variant converted for target towing duties as a TT18.

With a crew of three it was carrying out a low speed asymmetric flight test with one of its engines shut down, when it entered a spin and crashed into the sea on a south westerly heading a mile or so from Burton Bradstock at 2.30 pm on a lovely spring afternoon. At least two parachutes, those of the pilot and navigator were seen to deploy and the wearers were plucked from the water by an RN helicopter, but only one – Flt Lt Nicol – survived. The body of the other ejectee, Major Weaver (an American Exchange Officer serving with the RAF), was taken to the Weymouth & District Hospital mortuary and later transferred by the USAF authorities to one of their bases in East Anglia.

HMS *Dark Gladiator* and HMS *Shulton*, together with fishing vessels, all recovered wreckage on the day of the accident and the *Shulton* continued to search until 7th May, when she recovered an A13 flight data recorder, followed, shortly afterwards, by the other two recorders fitted to WJ632. Most of the data contained in these three 'black boxes' was electronically readable. The *MV Pintail* continued to operate at the scene of the accident until 14th May, by which time all major wreckage had been recovered and landed at Portland Naval Base.

3rd May 1970

McDonnell F-4 Phantom FG1; serial number XV566.

Pilot: Lt Alex Stewart.

Observer: Lt Phillip Coombes.

Unit: No 892 Sqn, FAA, embarked upon the aircraft carrier *HMS Ark Royal*.

The crew was acting as the target for a low level interception exercise under the control of *Ark Royal* when radio and radar contact was lost.

Despite a sea search by the frigates *HMSs Ashanti* and *Llandaff*, the patrol boat *HMS Dark Gladiator* and the minesweeper *HMS Soberton*, and an aerial search by helicopters and an RAF Shackleton, no trace of crew or aircraft could be found.

The search was abandoned on 5th May. No cause for the accident was ever established, but pilot disorientation was considered a possibility.

16th May 1983

Hawker Hunter GA11; serial number XE716.

Pilot: Mr Dan Carter.

Unit: Fleet Requirements and Air Direction Unit, RNAS Yeovilton.

Flown by a civilian pilot from the FRADU, a unit which was based at RNAS Yeovilton and provided the Armed Forces (primarily the Royal Navy) with target facilities, the aircraft crashed into the sea just two miles off Chesil Bank after an engine failure during an air-to-air interception exercise, for which it was acting as target aircraft.

The pilot ejected successfully, and was picked up from the water by a Wessex helicopter from RNAS Portland, piloted by Lt Ian Bryant, and ferried to the sick bay of *HMS Osprey*. His only injuries were minor ones to his back – a common problem following the stresses on the spine of an ejection.

The following week the wreckage of the Hunter, which had originally been delivered to the RAF as an F4 variant in October 1955, was recovered from the seabed by the Portland Dockyard's lifting vessel *RMAS Kinbrace*.

Today similar tasks to those which Mr Carter was carrying out in his Hunter, before his life was saved by his Martin Baker ejector seat, are carried out by FR Aviation's Dassault Falcon 20 twin-jet aircraft based, in Dorset, at Bournemouth International Airport, Hurn.

The mangled remains of FRADU Hunter XE716 lie deposited on the jetty at Portland awaiting collection for accident analysis. *RMAS Kinbrace* is tied up alongside.

Further Accidents For Which I Can Find No Supporting Documentation or Records

Mr Fred Foster tells me of two accidents, both sometime in 1945 and certainly before the cessation of hostilities:

1. A Spitfire that had been carrying out a gunnery exercise crash-landed alongside the range, with the wreckage later being taken away on an RAF low-loader lorry. (These lorries were known in RAF service as 'Queen Marys').

2. During a live rocket attack on one of the targets by an RAF Typhoon aircraft, the underwing rockets ignited but did not leave the aircraft, and the fighter-bomber crashed into the sea just offshore. The pilot was rescued by a passing fishing vessel before the range safety vessel reached the scene.

SEVEN

Wing Commander George Stainforth AFC

George Hedley Stainforth served as an Army officer before embarking upon a career in the Royal Air Force. A pupil at the former Weymouth College in Dorchester Road from 1915 to 1917, he graduated from Sandhurst Royal Military College in August 1918 and was appointed to a commission in the East Kent Regiment ("The Buffs"), with which regiment he served in India, Iraq and Aden. Stainforth retired from the Army in 1922 and a year later was awarded a Short Service Commission in the RAF.

His first operational appointment was to 19 Sqn, but he was short-toured there and selected in 1924 for training at the RAF's Central Flying School (CFS) as a flying instructor, going on to put his instructional skills to good use at No 4 Flying Training School at Abu Sueir (Abu Suweir) in Egypt's Canal Zone. His exceptional flying ability resulted in him returning to CFS as a staff instructor and as a member of the School's formation aerobatics team. He later set a world record for inverted flight (12 minutes), took part in the King's Cup Air Races and, being a crack shot, represented the RAF at Bisley with both rifle and revolver.

Stainforth's talents did not go unnoticed and in 1928, as a young officer who was obviously 'going places' in the RAF, he was posted to the RAF High Speed Flight at the Marine Aircraft Experimental Establishment, which had been formed at RAF Felixstowe on 1st October 1926, under the command of Sqn Ldr L.J. Slater. He was on strength when Sqn Ldr A.H. Orlebar took over command on 1st February 1929, with Flt Lt D.D'Arcy Greig, Fg Off R.L.R. Atcherley and Fg Off H.R.D. Waghorn as his fellow pilots, and Fg Off T.H. Moon as the Flight's engineering officer.

On 10th September 1929 he became the holder of the world air speed record, achieving a speed of 336.3 mph in the Gloster-Napier VI aircraft N249, 'Golden Arrow'. It was in this same year, flying as navigator to Atcherley, that the pair won the King's Cup Air Race.

In September 1927 Britain had won the tenth Schneider Trophy Contest at Venice (the first contest

Squadron Leader (later Wing Commander) George Hedley Stainforth in formal mess kit in the pre-war years. His Air Force Cross is the medal nearest to the button line on his tunic.[Photograph: RAF Strike Command/Ministry of Defence (Crown Copyright Reserved)]

had been flown off Monaco in March 1913) and had gone on to win the eleventh off Calshot two years later. The next contest – the twelfth – was in fact 'no contest', for neither the United States nor Italy was able to ready an aeroplane in time to compete and the British team needed only to fly a single aircraft around the course above the waters of the Solent off Calshot to claim victory and outright ownership of the Trophy itself.

The winning aircraft, the George Mitchell

designed Supermarine S6B floatplane S1595, was flown by Flt Lt J.N. Boothman at a speed of 340.08 mph (547.305 km/h). It was, of course, from the aircraft developed for the Schneider Trophy contests that the Supermarine Spitfire was developed and which flew for the first time from Eastleigh on 5th March 1936.

Under a gentleman's agreement, it had been decided whoever did not fly in the 1931 contest, would fly the aircraft selected to attempt to raise the World Air Speed Record. As Flt Lt Boothman had been chosen to pilot the aircraft for the fly-over in the 1931 'non race' (S1595), and Flt Lt Long and Fg Off Snaith had been selected as the two reserve pilots, the honour of piloting the record attempt aircraft fell upon the shoulders of George Stainforth.

On 13th September 1931, after the formalities of the race were over, he took off in the specially prepared S1596, the engine of which was tuned to run on a unique fuel mixture of petrol, ethyl and methanol, to raise the record from Sqn Ldr Orlebar's 1929 record of 357.7 mph to a new one of 379.05 mph. The aircraft is now on display at The Science Museum in London (together with the actual Schneider Trophy).

The magic figure of 400 mph now beckoned. S1595 had had a lot of work done on its Rolls Royce 'R' series engine and the fuel it burnt – the supercharger gearing ratio was raised and the fuel octane raised quite dramatically – whilst S1596 was used as the primary practice aircraft before the big day of the actual attempt to break the 'magic 400' threshold.

It was an incident in this aircraft on 16th September 1931 which nearly cost Stainforth his life. Just before 4.00 pm on this Wednesday afternoon he was coming in to land off Calshot at the usual high approach speed (for those days) of some 100 mph, when on touch down S1596 swerved off the landing line, the nose dipped and the seaplane overturned. Only the twin blue floats were visible on the sea's surface but, as three speed boats raced to the scene, Stainforth clambered out from below the aircraft and stood on one of the floats awaiting rescue – his only injuries being a badly cut nose and some bruises.

The enquiry into the accident concluded that he had caught his heel in the rudder bar (which was connected to both the flying rudder on the tailfin and the sea rudder) whilst correcting drift on touchdown, and that the sea rudder deflection had caused the aircraft to swerve off course and then tip over. The aircraft was recovered little damaged.

Waiting to board his aircraft at Calshot after pre-flight testing is complete, Stainforth appears to be in a far-off world of his own! Note the groundcrew personnel, wearing their waterproof beaching suits and life jackets, holding down the rear of the SN6 whilst engine ground runs are completed.

Engine tuning completed, Stainforth flew S1595 – resplendent in blue and silver markings – over six circuits of a set course on 29th September 1931 to set a new world speed record of 407.5 mph. Ten days later, in recognition of his considerable contribution to aviation (this was his third current record-breaking flight), he was awarded the Air Force Cross.

His 1931 record stood until 23rd October 1934, when it was broken by the Italian aviator Warrant Officer Francesco Agello with a speed of 440.68 mph in a twin-engined Macchi MC72 at Lake Garda – the world air speed record for a propeller driven seaplane which still stands today.

Following achieving his third world air speed record, Stainforth presented Weymouth College with a hardwood copper-sheathed wind vane, in the form of an S6B aircraft – the actual presentation being made in July 1932. The memento, mounted some 80 feet above ground level on the Victorian College Chapel, was designed by a Mr Pite – an uncle of the Headmaster – and in 1940, when the college closed, it was taken down for safe keeping and presented to the Borough Council.

Eighty feet up, George Stainforth (right) poses for the camera on the day of the installation of the Supermarine S6B wind vane on Weymouth College chapel in 1932. As have the main educational buildings next to it, it has now been converted into a private residence.

Stainforth next served at the Royal Aircraft Establishment, Farnborough, as a test pilot, where he was especially involved with testing the revolutionary Westland-Hill Pterodactyl flying wing types of aircraft. In April 1933, he made the very first flight in the Airspeed AS5 Courier five seat passenger aircraft. Apart from one experimental Bristol aircraft at the end of the Great War, the Courier was the first British aircraft to fly with a retractable undercarriage, which gave no trouble in these early flights. However, the single radial engine did occasionally give Stainforth the odd scare – most especially when it failed completely at 300 feet over Langstone Harbour after an easterly direction take-off from Portsmouth Airport (where Airspeed was based) and required all of the aviator's skill and expertise to execute an emergency turn back for a safe downwind landing.

The previous year he had had another in-flight emergency requiring him to test his flying ability to the limit, when the propeller of the single-engine aircraft which he was flying several thousand feet above Reading snapped off at the hub. Stainforth was able to glide down safely for a 'dead stick' landing. The detached section of the propeller fell into a field at Holly Cross Farm, Bramley, where it was later found by two farm labourers and handed to the police for forwarding to Farnborough for detailed examination.

Life is full of little coincidences, and here we find one tied to the former Chickerell airfield site. As we have seen, two of the streets on the old airfield are named Cobham Drive and Stainforth Close: one of the directors of Airspeed (later its Managing Director) was Sir Alan Cobham, and the test pilot he selected for the Courier test flights was none other than George Stainforth!

On Friday 30th May 1952, with Mayor, other civic dignitaries and Stainforth's two brothers in attendance, the commemorative wind vane was erected atop a memorial plinth in Weymouth's Greenhill Gardens. In 1996, battered by its continuous exposure to the salt air and winter gales of Weymouth Bay, the vane was taken down for major renovation by local classic car enthusiast Jim Avery and, virtually rebuilt 'from scratch', it was re-erected there in June three years later.

The text on the plinth below the stone column reads: 'This weathervane commemorates the establishment of a world speed record of 406.92 mph (*sic*) on 29th September 1931 by Flight Lieutenant G.H. Stainforth AFC, an old boy of Weymouth College and a member of the Schneider Trophy Team. The aircraft of which this is a replica was the prototype (*sic*) of the Battle of Britain

Stainforth Memorial, Greenhill Gardens, Weymouth: detail of memorial plinth.

THIS WEATHERVANE COMMEMORATES THE ESTABLISHMENT OF A WORLD SPEED RECORD OF 406·92 M.P.H. ON THE 29TH SEPTEMBER 1931 BY FLIGHT LIEUTENANT G.H. STAINFORTH A.F.C AN OLD BOY OF WEYMOUTH COLLEGE AND A MEMBER OF THE SCHNEIDER TROPHY TEAM THE AIRCRAFT OF WHICH THIS IS A REPLICA WAS THE PROTOTYPE OF THE BATTLE OF BRITAIN 'SPITFIRE'. ORIGINALLY ERECTED OVER THE COLLEGE IN JULY 1932 THE VANE WAS PRESENTED TO THE BOROUGH WHEN THE COLLEGE CLOSED IN 1940 AND WAS MOUNTED IN ITS PRESENT POSITION IN MAY 1952

Above The post-war rededication of the Stainforth Memorial. Gathered around the Portland stone column are the Mayor (Cllr L James), Deputy Mayor (Cllr A. Medlam), the Mace Bearer (Mr W. Damen), Mayor's Chaplain (Revd M. Garner) and Town Clerk (Mr P. Smallman). The stocky gentleman carrying his trilby is Revd Edward Tanner, MC, Chaplain and Housemaster at Weymouth College in George Stainforth's days as a student, whilst the gentleman facing the camera to his left is almost certainly one of the two Stainforth brothers present.

Right Stainforth Memorial: detail of wind vane.

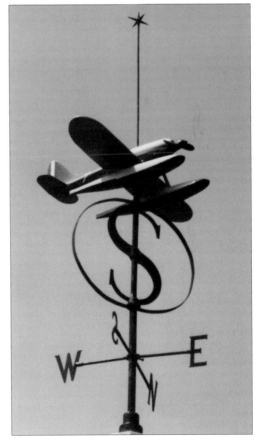

Spitfire. Originally erected over the college in July 1932, the vane was presented to the Borough when the College closed in 1940 and was mounted in its present position in May 1952.'

There appear to be two errors in the text on the plinth:

1. All official records show the record speed to have been 407.5 mph.
2. The aircraft was the forerunner or inspiration for the Spitfire; it was not the prototype.

After his record-breaking slighhts, and now promoted to Squadron Leader, Stainforth next served with the Fleet Air Arm on the carrier *HMS Glorious* and in Iraq at Hinaidi and, next, at

Habbaniyah – where he commanded No 30 Squadron, equipped from January 1938 with Blenheim light bombers.

On Empire Day, May 1939 he made headlines by flying a Spitfire from the south of England to Scotland and back at an average speed of 273 mph (437 km/h). Then, during the dark years of 1939 and 1940, he was in command of the Aircraft Handling Flight at the Central Flying School – a critically important job, of both tactical and technical importance to front line units as they fought for Britain's very existence.

Indicative of the high esteem in which he was held, it was Stainforth who was chosen in 1940, whilst at CFS (based at RAF Upavon on Salisbury Plain), to report to Farnborough to fly a captured Me109 in mock combat against Flt Lt (later Wg Cdr) Bob Stanford-Tuck to ascertain the German fighter's characteristics and to devise counter tactics – which were to prove invaluable during The Battle of Britain. Initially Stainforth flew the Me 109 and Stanford-Tuck the Spitfire and then the Hurricane, before the two pilots changed their steeds for the second portion of the trials. Their opinion was that the Me109 was slightly faster than the Spitfire (the quicker of the two British aircraft flown against it),

Personnel of No 89 Squadron, probably at Abu Sueir, display the unit's 'Kill Board' – utilising the national markings of a downed German aircraft. Wg Cdr Stainforth is prominent in the centre of the group; looking over his left shoulder (full face) is Fg Off 'Pete' Lawton, his navigator/airborne intercept radar operator.

but not as agile.

Also with his CFS hat on, Stainforth was instrumental in restoring the confidence of pilots flying the Blenheim aircraft, employed as a medium bomber and as a stop-gap night fighter, in the reliability of the aeroplane's twin Mercury radial engines and engine-out performance – mainly by demonstrating better pre and post take-off engine handling techniques.

Newly promoted to Wing Commander, Stainforth's next appointment was to command of No 600 Squadron, which was operating Bristol Beaufighters in the night fighter role, his first claimed 'probable' kill being for a Heinkel He111 shot down on 7th April. He then took command of the forming-up No 89 Squadron at RAF Colerne (near Bath), which was preparing to serve overseas – again with Beaufighters in the NF role – and oversaw the ferrying of the initial allocation of aircraft to North

Beaufighter NF Mk 1, in the same black camouflage as the Stainforth/Lawson X7700 would have carried. There is an axiom in aviation: 'If an aircraft looks good, it will be good', and this could certainly be said of the Beaufighter.

In July 1942 Prime Minister Winston Churchill visited Egypt to find out first hand what problems were besetting the British Military machine in its attempts to oust Field Marshal Edwin Rommel's Afrika Corps from North Africa. Here we see Wg Cdr Stainforth escorting the VIP party, probably at Abu Seir. To Churchill's left walks Air Vice Marshal Arthur Tedder, Air Commander Middle East (and later Eisenhower's Deputy Supreme Allied Commander for the assault landings in North West Europe), whilst the taller of the two Army officers behind him is General Sir Claude Auchinleck – soon to be replaced in post by General Bernard Montgomery. Anthony Eden, the British Foreign Secretary is the other civilian in the party, and the aircraft is a VIP configured Lockheed Hudson, developed from the Lockheed Electra airliner, but operating here as originally conceived.

Africa, via Portreath, Gibraltar and Malta, and its new base at Stainforth's old stomping ground of Abu Sueir.

During the hours of darkness of Saturday 4th/Sunday 5th July 1942, Stainforth was one of three 89 Sqn pilots credited with a night kill, when he shot down a Junkers JU88 which fell in flames near to the town of Damietta, on the Egyptian coast to the west of Port Said.

The oldest pilot on operations in North Africa Theatre (he was 43 years old), Stainforth rarely rested and, sadly, this may have been a factor in his death, and that of his long-standing navigator and good friend Fg Off 'Pete' Lawson, on 27th September 1942. At 1740 hours, they departed from Abu Sueir in Beaufighter X7700 (Sugar) to the airstrip at Ras Gharib, about 130 miles south of Suez, to hold the 'Night Readiness State' and were scrambled at 2200 hours on a defensive patrol, during which they suffered a failure of one of the aircraft's Hercules XVII engines and returned

towards the airstrip, which had virtually no night flying facilities. It would seem that the aircraft possibly suffered a second engine failure – maybe due to fuel starvation – and that the crew were killed after bailing out too low for their parachutes to open properly.

Thus Wing Commander George Stainforth AFC's remarkable flying career came to a close, and he lies buried at the Commonwealth War Graves Commission Cemetery at Ismailia, Egypt. In addition to the monument in Greenhill Gardens, he is commemorated locally on a plaque in St Aldhelm's Church, Spa Road, Radipole.

No 89 Squadron itself was disbanded on 1st May 1946 at Seletar, Singapore, to become No 22 Squadron, which is currently one of the RAF's two front line Search and Rescue helicopter squadrons (the other is 202 Sqn), now operating the twin-engine Sea King HAR3 and HAR4 out of six UK airfields.

The George Stainforth Trophy

The George Stainforth Trophy was presented to RAF Strike Command on 7th June 1974 by the No 89 Squadron Reunion Club, its cost being met by an anonymous donor (later known to have been the late Mrs Stella Sketch), and commemorates the long and distinguished career of Wg Cdr Stainforth as both an exceptional aviator and an RAF officer.

The trophy, designed by Mr Robin Beresford, portrays the earth as seen from space: vapour trails ending in arrows to depict high speed flight, swept outwards to infinity to suggest that the sky is, quite

The George Stainforth Trophy. [Photograph: RAF Strike Command/Ministry of Defence (Crown Copyright Reserved)]

literally, the limit of mankind's achievement in the air. The trophy has incorporated in it a star, and its orbit evokes memories of the achievements of science, and of the Royal Air Force motto *Per Ardua Ad Astra* – 'Through Hardship to the Stars'.

The trophy, first presented jointly to RAF Coltishall and RAF Patrington for their achievements in 1973 and considered one of the most prestigious trophies which can grace an RAF Station's silver cabinet, is awarded annually by the Air Officer Commanding Strike Command to an operational station within the Command, recognising both its operational excellence and its contribution to the RAF as a whole.

The 2001 recipient was RAF Waddington in Lincolnshire, home to No 8 and No 23 Squadron, which operate the Boeing E-3D Sentry aircraft in the airborne early warning, command and control role, and No 51 Squadron which operates the BAe Nimrod R1 in the electronic reconnaissance and electronic combat support roles.

The 2002 recipient was RAF Odiham, the home of the RAF's Chinook helicopter force, for the support given to the station's global commitments throughout the year. Its three Chinook squadrons' worked in support of operations on a worldwide scale, most especially – but by no means exclusively – in operations against Al Q'aida in Afghanistan and ranged as far across the globe as Northern Ireland, the Falkland Islands, mainland Europe and the Middle East.

In 2003 the trophy went to RAF Marham, in Suffolk, home to No II, IX (B), XIII and 31 Squadrons, operating the Tornado GR4 and No 39 (1 PRU) Squadron which operates the Canberra PR 7 – the only RAF squadron still flying this venerable twin jet (which first flew on 13th May 1949). The

The Stainforth Memorial today – still standing proudly in Weymouth's Greenhill Gardens.

The 2002 Stainforth Trophy is presented by Air Chief Marshal Sir John Day KCB, OBE, ADC, BSc, RAF, Commander-In-Chief of RAF Strike Command (left) to Group Captain Andy Pulford RAF, the RAF Odiham Station Commander. [Photograph: RAF Strike Command/Ministry of Defence (Crown Copyright Reserved)]

award was given in recognition of the station's operational efficiency across a wide spectrum of operational and training tasks – most especially Operations *Telic* and *Fresco*, earned against a background of numerous other tasks, both in the air and in support of the community at large. Her Majesty the Queen is Honorary Air Commodore to RAF Marham.

The most recent staion to win the coveted award was RAF Kinloss, the Nimrod base on the Moray Firth coastline, in Scotland – home to 120 and 201 Sqns and 42 (Reserve) Sqn, a Mountain Rescue Team and the UK's Aeronautical Rescue Co-Ordination Centre. The trophy was awarded for operations in The Gulf, Afganistan, the Carribean and for activities at home, including numerous long-range search and rescue missions. It was presented to Group Captain Chris Birks, Officer Commanding, by the Commander-in-Chief RAF Strike Command, Air Chief Marshal Sir Brian Burridge, himself a former Station Commander at Kinloss. Kinloss Nimrods are occasionally to be seen in local skies, both exercising with the Royal Navy and carrying out operations in support of HM Customs.

Acknowledgements

Mrs Maureen Attwooll, Mrs Jenni Aram, the late Sqn Ldr Chris Ashworth, Wg Cdr Terry Bacon, Mr Aubrey Bell, Mr Bill Bork, Mr Bill & Mrs Pat Clancy Mr 'Gonga' Clapson, Wg Cdr Derek Collier Webb, Mr Ron Connor, Mr Brian Cook, Mr Anthony Cooke, Mr Ralph Cooper, Mr & Mrs Charlie Cox, Mr Jack Cranny, Mr Nicholas Dicks, Mr Neville Doyle, Mr Mike Ellis, Mr Peter Elmer, Gp Capt Derek Empson MBE, Mr John Evans, Mr Fred Foster, Mr Alan Fowler, Mr Douglas Gardner, Mr Dennis German, Mr Clinton Grassby, Mr Peter Hamilton, Mr John Hamlin, Mr Frederick Harker, Mr Douglas Homer, Mr Keith Hooper, Mr Brian Jackson, Mrs Helen Lambie, Mr Guy Jefferson, Mr Jack Jones, Sqn Ldr Peter Jones, Mr John Joyce, Mrs Helen Lambie, Mr David Lane, the late Mr George Lanning, Mr Sid Legg, Mrs Joy Luxton, Mr Frank Marshall, Mr Edward McBride, Mr Ian MacNab, Air Cdre Andrew Neal AFC, Sqn Ldr Alan Nicoll, Sqn Ldr Bernard Noble, Mr Robert Owen, Mr Reg Perry, WO Bill Pitcher, Mr Peter Price, Mr Peter C Price, Mr Geoffrey Pritchard, Mr Mike Reed, Major Peter Reed, Wg Cdr Jim Routledge, Mr Robert Russell, Mr Richard Samways, Mr Alan Scholefield, Mr Donald Smith, Mr Duncan Smith, Mr Peter Stainforth, Mr D Stevens, Mr Harold Tonkins, Mr Ray Towler, Mrs Rosemary Waring, Mr Max Warwick, Mr Brian Whitehead, Mr Roy White, Mt Stuart Whyte, Mr Dennis Willes, Mr Selwyn Williams, Mr 'Woody' Williams, Mr Norman Wilson, Mr Frank Windale, and Mr Ted Woods.

British Airways, Channel 4 'Service Pals', The Dorset County Records Office, The Dorset Echo (most especially The Wanderer and Mr Mike Clarke), The Fleet Air Arm Museum, Lyme Regis Museum, The Public Libraries at Dorchester & Weymouth, The Public Records Office, The Royal Air Force Museum, The Royal Air Force Air Defence Radar Museum, The Royal Aeronautical Society, The Brewers Quay Museum Archives Section, The Southampton Hall of Aviation, No 89 Squadron & No 617 Squadron Aircrew Associations.

Finally, I am particularly indebted to Alan Smith, MRAeS, and Colin Cruddas for their many helpful suggestions and invaluable advice.

To any person or organisation from whom I have received assistance but have unintentionally omitted from the listing above, I extend both my apologies and my thanks.

I am extremely grateful to the following who have so kindly made available to me the photographs in the book: No 89 Squadron Association, No 203 (R) Squadron Archives, No 619 Squadron Archives, the late Sqn Ldr R.C.B. Ashworth, Maureen Attwool, J Beedle (via R.A. Scholefield), Davis Bidgood, Blackburn Aircraft Company, Brewers Quay Museum, Wg Cdr John Bussey MBE, The Coastal Command and Maritime Air Association (via Paul Warrener), 'Gonga' Clapson (via Roy White), HM Coastguard, Charles Cox, Cobham plc, Colin Cruddas, Dorset & Somerset Air Ambulance, Dors et Echo, Dorset Police, Mark Ellis, Flt Lt Neville Feist, John Fidlin (via John Evans), Fleet Air Arm Museum, Katherine Foote, Douglas Gardner, Mr D.E.B. German, Andy Hutchings, AT Jackson Collection, Brian Jackson, R.J. Jackson, L. Kestin (via Colin Caddy), Mrs J. Luxton, Frank Marshall, Roy O'Connor, *HMS Osprey*, Peter Price, W.J. Pitcher (via his son Warrant Officer W. Pitcher), the late Air Cdr 'Taffy' Powell (via his son David Powell), RAF Strike Command/Ministry of Defence, Southampton Hall of Aviation, the late Lionel Vart, Jack West, Weymouth Library, Brian Whitehead, Mr H. Willes, and Selwyn Williams.

Bibliography

Ashford, R.C.B., *Action Stations, Volume 5* (1982, 1990).
Chickerell Parish Council, *Chickerell "Yer Tiz"*.
Cooke, A, *Reflections of RAF Warmwell* (2000).
Cruddas, C, *In Cobhams' Company* (1994).
   Cobham. The Flying Years (1997).
   In Dorset's Skies (2000).
Dawson, L., *Wings Over Dorset* (1983 & 1989).
Hamlin, J., *Peaceful Fields*.
Jackson, A.J., *British Civil Aircraft 1919 – 1972* (3 Vols), 1973.
Jefford, C., *Royal Air Force Squadrons* (1988).
Lake, A., *Flying Units of the RAF* (1999).
Mondey, D., *The Schneider Trophy*, (1975).
Pereira, W., *Boat In The Blue*, (1985).
Pomeroy, C., *Military Dorset Today*, (1995).
Shute, N., *Slide Rule* (1954).
Sturtivant, R. & Ballance, T., *The Squadrons of the Fleet Air Arm* (1994).